THE BIG UMBRELLA

JOHN LUCAS

The Big Umbrella

*THE HISTORY OF THE PARACHUTE
FROM DA VINCI TO APOLLO*

WITH A FOREWORD BY
GROUP CAPTAIN DOUGLAS BADER
CBE, DSO, DFC

ELM TREE BOOKS
HAMISH HAMILTON LONDON

First published in Great Britain 1973
by Elm Tree Books Ltd
90 Great Russell Street London WC1

Copyright © 1973 by John Lucas

SBN 241 02294 0

Printed in Great Britain by
Western Printing Services Ltd, Bristol

To my Mother and Father

'*Parachute:* Umbrella-like apparatus for descending safely from a height, esp. from aircraft'—
Oxford English Dictionary

CONTENTS

ACKNOWLEDGEMENTS

To the many people who generously gave of their time and expertise during my researches for this book, my warm gratitude. I appreciate especially the invaluable help of Mr Charles Gibbs-Smith, the eminent aeronautical historian, for guidance on the parachute's early history, and for reading through the relevant chapters of my manuscript.

My thanks, too, to Mr A. W. Nayler, librarian of the Royal Aeronautical Society, and his assistant, Mrs E. Dane, for their interest and suggestions, and loans of material: and to Dr Christopher Dowling and his colleagues of the Imperial War Museum.

I am also indebted to the following: Mrs Velda Irvin, of Los Angeles, whose late husband, Leslie L. Irvin, made the first modern free-fall jump and founded the company which bears his name, for checking and enlarging upon details of her husband's life; Mr Leslie Pargeter, late of the Royal Flying Corps, who supplied me with personal reminiscences on flying without parachutes in World War I; Mrs Renée Hampshire, for background material concerning her father, Major Orde-Lees, who strove to obtain parachutes for Mr Pargeter and his ill-fated colleagues; Wing-Commander J. Jewell, of Martin-Baker Ltd, for his guidance on the development of the British ejection seat; Air Vice-Marshal Donald Bennett, former leader of the RAF's Pathfinder Force, who kindly described for me the parachute's role in air operations over Germany: my friend Eric Stevens, for personal recollections of paratroop warfare; Squadron Leader W. Paul, Secretary-general, British Parachute Association; Mr John Meacock, British parachute jumping champion; Squadron Leader Ronald Smith, of No. 1 Parachute Training School, RAF Abingdon; and Miss Joan Walthew, whose scrapbooks and other material relating to parachutes in World War II proved most valuable; Mr John Simpson, managing director, and individual members of the staff of Irvin Great Britain Ltd, particularly Mr Gordon Eastley, and their public relations adviser, Miss Shirley Koster; members of the staff of RFD–GQ Ltd, and in particular, Mr Arthur C. Dickinson, formerly joint managing director; Northrop-Ventura Ltd, U.S.A.; the U.S. Dept of Agriculture; the National Aeronautics and Space Administration, Washington DC; Mr Malcolm Lumb, of Cable & Wireless; the British Meteorological Office; and members of the staffs of the British Museum and its Newspaper Library, the National Library of Science and Invention, and the Patent Office Library, for their usual unstinting help.

Lastly, my affectionate thanks to my wife for her assistance and support in innumerable ways, and her constant encouragement when the canopy of thought occasionally failed to deploy.

J.L.

Transcripts of Crown copyright records in the Public Records Office appear by permission of the Controller of H.M. Stationery Office; the extract from *Years of Command* by Lord Douglas of Kirtleside and R. C. Wright appears by permission of A. D. Peters & Co., and the extract from *The German Air Force in the Great War* by G. P. Neumann is reproduced by permission of Times Newspapers Ltd.

For permission to reproduce the photographs in this book, the author wishes to thank:
Irvin Great Britain Ltd
U.S. Forest Service
Daily Mirror
Daily Telegraph
N.A.S.A., Washington
David Waterman Esq.
National Library of Science and Invention, London
Messrs RFG–GQ
British Museum

Imperial War Museum
Royal Aeronautical Society
T. W. Willans Esq.
Martin-Baker Ltd
Mrs Renée Hampshire

FOREWORD

by Group Captain Douglas Bader CBE, DSO, DFC

I congratulate John Lucas on this splendid book. It is the first time
in my recollection that anyone has attempted to write a history
of the parachute from its early days. Indeed, I did not know that
its history went back two hundred years, and I am quite sure no
one else has realised this. I found this book fascinating and tremen-
dously readable; it also contains much humour without which
a book like this would not reach print.

Although the parachute itself did not come into existence until
two hundred years ago, John Lucas has discovered some fascinating performances, even before the time of Leonardo da Vinci in
the fifthteenth century. I especially like the story of the Turk who
announced that he would fly a furlong from the top of a high
tower. His aeronautical device consisted of 'a long and large white
garment, gathered into many plaits and foldings made on purpose
for gathering of the wind'. He had obviously done his sums
incorrectly, because his attempt proved fatally unsuccessful.

In the last few months of World War I, the Germans sprang a
great surprise on the Allied flyers by introducing a successful parachute, and saved many of their airmen's lives. Through the usual
bureaucratic mishandling, delay and indecision, British flyers were
not equipped with parachutes until some years after 1918. In
World War II, the parachute saved countless lives.

I commend this book to the reader. It is a combination of historical fact and amusing anecdote.

London SW7   DB
January 1973

YESTERDAY'S DREAMS

FREUD MIGHT have read a world of meaning into the billowing white canopy of the parachute. Protective mother, guardian angel, gentle virgin pure and unsullied, or sacred mushroom?

Certainly, during its two-hundred-year history, it has meant many things to many men: lifetimes have been devoted to the cause of its improvement, and many lives sacrificed in the testing of the various prototypes. For scores of thousands, succoured by food and medical supplies which floated down to them in peace and war, it was as welcome as manna from heaven. Indeed, the parachute has even been to the heavens and back, for when man tired of this world and began casting around space for others to catch his fancy, the parachute was there, as always, to bring him back home and let him down lightly.

According to Greek mythology, the ingenious inventor Daedalus made wings for himself and his son, Icarus, so that they could escape from the labyrinth in Crete in which they were held captive by King Minos. Icarus foolishly ignored his father's warning not to fly too near the sun; as a result, the wax which attached his wings to his body melted and he fell to his death. One would like to gild this story with a happy ending, but although Icarus bridged the gap between earth and the heavens, he had no parachute to ensure his return! It was man who was to devise a means of escape from the hazards of the air: the parachute's place was in reality, not myth.

The parachute's development ran in parallel with man's yearning to fly, yet experimentation preceded flight with a heavier-than-air machine by several decades. It was a painful, often fatal, struggle for perfection, but one which has been amply repaid: this basically simple device, an echo of nature's reach-me-down parachute, the dandelion seed, and the spider's airborne gossamer, has saved 200,000 lives, according to Charles H. Gibbs-Smith, the aeronautical historian.

Yet so distant in time are its origins that the parachute's story hardly has a beginning; nor, in the space age, is it over. The parasol, which was in use in Assyria 2,800 years ago, is thought to have inspired the parachute, no doubt because of the resistance it was found to offer to a brisk wind. Yet not until the eighteenth century, when man began to take to the air in balloons, did the aeronautical possibilities become apparent.

Tragedy has been a constant companion of the parachute. One of the first of many disasters occurred in Constantinople in 1147, so we understand from Knolles's *General History of the Turks*. Emanuel, the Greek Emperor, was being visited by the Turkish Sultan Clisasthan, one of whose retinue had spread the word that at a given time and place—the tiltyard—he would fly a furlong from the top of a high tower. He had no parachute, but 'a long and large white garment, gathered into many plaits and foldings, made on purpose for gathering of the wind'. It was not enough: despite the Emperor's entreaties not to tempt Providence, the Turk leapt off the tower and broke every bone in his body.

In his book *A New Historical Relation of the Kingdom of Siam*, Simon de la Loubère, who was French ambassador in Siam in the 1680s, relates how a tumbler jumped from 'the hoop' with two umbrellas fixed to his girdle: 'the wind carry'd him accidentally sometimes to the Ground, sometimes on Trees or Houses, and sometimes into the River. He so exceedingly diverted the King of Siam that this Prince had made him a great Lord: he had lodged him in the Palace and had given him a great Title; or, as they say, a great Name.'

The earliest parachutes were a pyramid-shaped type sketched by Leonardo da Vinci, and a conical one drawn by an unknown artist whose work is preserved in the British Museum, both dating from the 1480s. They are thought to have derived from an earlier and common source not yet discovered.

The conical parachute of the anonymous artist shows a figure holding on to a wooden crosspiece spanning its mouth. A second drawing, of a totally unconvincing fall-breaker, depicts a similar figure clutching two long ribbon-like strips of cloth which flutter above his head.

Leonardo's pyramid-like parachute was drawn in 1485 and appears in the Codex Atlanticus. A translation of his description reads: 'If a man has a tent roof of caulked linen twelve braccia broad and twelve braccia high, he will be able to let himself fall from any great height without danger to himself.'

A braccia approximated to a yard, so Da Vinci's device would have measured about 36 feet wide and 36 feet from base to apex. The canopy would have stretched over a wooden framework and from the apex there would be a pole. From this the jumper would have hung, clutching a cord from each corner.

Whether Leonardo ever made an experimental model is not known, but a lifesize version, given these dimensions and the use of light wood, would almost certainly have provided sufficient drag through the air to bring a man down safely. The modern man-carrying parachute, almost a precision instrument with its array of slits and apertures which act as aerofoils for manoeuvrability, has a flat diameter varying between 24 and 28 feet.

Leonardo cannot be called the true originator of the parachute because it was centuries before his drawings and other writings re-emerged from obscurity. When he died, near Amboise in France in 1519, he left all his manuscripts to the supposedly safe keeping of his friend Francesco da Melzi. Either through ignorance or carelessness, Melzi stored them away for half a century, on his own death leaving them to his son, who cared nothing at all for their importance, even supposing he recognised it.

Despite this monumental piece of offhandedness, most of Leonardo's precious drawings and notes have been preserved, though some did fall into other hands. Not until towards the end of the nineteenth century was a selection of his aeronautical sketches published, including his design for the parachute, and then only for limited circulation among academics. However, about a century earlier, in 1784, the Frenchman Jean-Pierre Blanchard had used the parachute in experiments for dropping animals, which proves beyond doubt that Leonardo's paper dreams for the parachute were, historically, redundant.

After Leonardo, no developments took place until 1595, when a Hungarian mathematician, Fausto Veranzio of Venice, published a book called *Machinae Novae*, which contained an engraving of '*Homo volans*' ('flying man') who appeared to be jumping from a tower, suspended from a square sheet on a stiff frame with a cord from each corner. Veranzio's suggestion that the size of the frame should be varied according to the weight of the 'cargo' showed an early grasp of sound principles, for in general the bigger the canopy the greater the drag and the greater the weight that can be sustained.

Had Veranzio ever seen Leonardo's sketch? It seems unlikely, for although his idea is reminiscent of Leonardo's, the execution is quite different. Leonardo drew a pyramid: Veranzio a sail-like sheet. Veranzio's 'sail' theme was taken up several times subsequently; for example, Des Maretz's *Ariane* (1639) contains an illustration of a prisoner escaping from a fortress by jumping and clutching the corners of a bed-sheet.

The first use of a parachute in an air machine was by Canon Desforges, of Etampes, in 1772. This ambitious but ill-named contraption, the 'voiture volant', was made of wicker-work and had wings worked by hand. Above hung a giant cloth canopy which, it was hoped, would help to keep it in the air. Desforges was in fact slightly injured when he tried it out from a tower. Nine years later, Blanchard made his 'flying ship', which was to be steered by a rudder motivated by movements of the body, and incorporating a parachute. Unfortunately, it never took to the air.

The invention of a parachute which could land a living being safely was taken a stage further in 1782 and 1783 with the invention of the hot-air balloon by two French brothers, Stephen and Joseph Montgolfier. Shortly before this, however, one of them, Joseph, an experimenter in other branches of aeronautics besides balloons, had investigated the principle of air-resistance, which a parachute of course employs, and he is reported to have safely descended with one from a housetop in Annonay, near Lyons, and dropped a sheep wearing a parachute from a tower at Avignon in 1779.

Being manufacturers by trade, the Montgolfier brothers had abundant material at their disposal for their successful 'fire balloon' experiments. They began by inflating small paper bags, and then a large silk bag, with hot air produced by burning chopped straw and wool. At first, they failed to understand what it was that made the balloon rise; they were convinced that it was due to 'gas' given off by the straw and wool burning beneath it rather than the warm air becoming lighter than the cold air outside.

They made two experimental balloons, one of which rose to about 600 feet. The second, made of paper-lined linen, ascended to 1,000 feet on April 25, 1783, and came down three-quarters of a mile away. On June 5, the brothers gave a public demonstration with a larger balloon, 110 feet in circumference and with a capacity of 22,000 cubic feet; it was so buoyant that eight men were needed to hold it down. Thousands of people from the surrounding countryside poured into Annonay to watch the ascent.

In the meantime, three others, Jacques Charles, a physicist, and the two brothers Robert, had perfected a way of making balloons which could use hydrogen rather than hot air. They had constructed a balloon from rubberised fabric and filled it with hydrogen produced by pouring sulphuric acid onto iron filings. On August 26 of 1783, the balloon rose 100 feet into the air, and on the following day a public display was given at the Champ de Mars on the site of what is now the Eiffel Tower. The balloon ascended 3,000 feet and came down fifteen miles away only to be torn to ribbons by frightened villagers at Gonesse.

On September 14, the Montgolfier brothers released their first-ever live balloonists from the Palace of Versailles: a sheep, a cock and a duck. History was made again with a nobler cargo two months later on November 21, when two volunteers, François Pilâtre de Rozier and the Marquis d'Arlandes, became the first men in 'space'. This trip was particularly hazardous, for as they rose from the Bois de Boulogne, in their circular wicker gallery, they had to contend with smoke and blasts of heat from the burning wool and straw which provided the hot air. It licked continually at the edges of the balloon's fabric, which had to be doused repeatedly with water. They descended unharmed five miles away, from a reputed height of 3,000 feet, about twenty-five minutes later, to a well-earned and enthusiastic reception.

Now followed a spate of parachute experiments. In 1783 Sebastien Lenormand, a French doctor, caused a sensation by constructing a 14-feet diameter cone-shaped parachute of cloth or oiled silk and jumping from the tower of Montpellier Observatory. In the same year he is said to have demonstrated from the windows of a house that a parachute could be used to escape from fire. An English balloonist, Thomas Martyn, published a paper in 1784 entitled 'Hints on Aerostatic Globes', in which he included a theoretical design for a navigable balloon fitted with sails, a rudder, and beneath it 'an Umbrella to afford an easy descent, should the balloon burst', which he claimed was similar to the one he had shown to the Prince of Wales a year earlier.

One fiasco of an attempt to make a parachute descent took place in August 1785, when another Englishman, Stuart Amos Arnold, a one-time naval purser, ascended from St George's Fields, London, in the balloon Royal George, which had an open silk parachute fixed underneath. On a large flat basket beneath the parachute lay Arnold's assistant George Appleby, who according to advance publicity would drop from a mile above the earth.

Disaster overtook the project only seconds after the launching. The balloon hit some railings and lurched into the sky without Appleby and Arnold senior, but with Arnold's son. The balloon, which was over-inflated, burst, and the envelope shot up into the net, slowing the descent. The boy was thrown out into the Thames practically unharmed. For the first time but not the last a parachute had been created by the balloon itself.

In France, more was being heard of the balloonist Jean-Pierre Blanchard, a man whose personality was less distinguished than some of his achievements. Though he was not short of courage, he had streaks of vanity, jealousy, and, when it suited him, deceitfulness. Blanchard was born in Normandy in 1753. His parents were poor, and although he received little education he did possess a natural talent for mechanics. He is said to have built a mechanical carriage, and travelled in it, at the age of six, invented a rat trap and constructed a velocipede at sixteen, and, at twenty-nine, to have made an elaborate device for raising the waters of the Seine.

On February 27, 1784, for a balloon ascent from Paris, Blanchard fitted a parachute over the car; however this, combined with the wings and rudder, were far more than the balloon could manage; five days later he made his first ascent from the Champ de Mars without them.

The next month Blanchard went up in an air balloon from Paris and descended near Sèvres. On this occasion he carried paddles (today considered to have performed no useful aeronautical function whatever) and an equally useless rudder.

When visiting England in 1784 and 1785, Blanchard revived his interest in parachutes. Blanchard quarrelled with Martyn, whose 'Hints on Aerostatic Globes' with its design for a balloon with an 'umbrella' attachment aroused Blanchard's anger. Through the medium of the press he sent Martyn a jeering letter claiming that he had invented the device himself, adding disdainfully: 'As to its being adapted to air balloons, let the discovery be yours: experience has convinced me that it can answer no manner of purpose.'

Martyn preferred to sidestep the implied invitation to retaliate and merely explained that the only originality he claimed was the parachute's adaptation to balloon use.

On June 3, 1785, Blanchard experimented with a silk parachute 20 feet in diameter dropped from a balloon above his much-vaunted but short-lived Balloon and Parachute Aerostatic Academy in Vauxhall. Two weeks later he tried to repeat the experiment with a sheep, but the demonstration failed, and he was forced to give frustrated spectators their money back. In subsequent experiments he used a dog as a passenger, then two years later made a parachute large enough to suspend a man or large

animal, though there seems to be some doubt as to whether he
had sufficient faith in it to try it out himself.

Blanchard was fond of dropping animals wearing parachutes.
This contemporary account, published in the *Journal de Paris* in
1785 describes his ascent from Lille on August 26 of that year and
gives a fascinating glimpse of the hero-worship accorded to
aeronauts in those days, particularly a publicity-conscious man
like Blanchard:

> Monsieur Blanchard had completed the filling of the balloon
> at 9.45 a.m. and he then applied himself to the various prepara-
> tions for the departure and the testing of the parachute. At
> 10.45 he entered the car with the Chevalier de l'Epinard, at
> which juncture the people who were assembled on the esplanade
> —the point of departure—cheered and applauded heartily. At
> 10.55 a.m. the ropes were cut and the balloon rose majestically
> into the sky. The aeronauts waved to the onlookers with their
> flags on which the arms of the town were painted. The balloon
> travelled southwards as it ascended, the wind being north-
> westerly. After four minutes the balloon was seen to sink a few
> fathoms and rise as quickly. At this point Monsieur Blanchard
> released the parachute, to which a dog was fastened, which
> seemed to fall very slowly; the dog came down three-quarters
> of a league from the town, quite unharmed. . . The balloon was
> in sight for three-quarters of an hour. . . There is no need to
> describe the feelings of the public at the moment that the
> balloon lifted off; they differed in no way from those of all men
> of sensibility.

A lavish reception, and even more substantial rewards, were in
store for the two aeronauts:

> M. Blanchard and the Chevalier de l'Epinard came down at
> 6 p.m. at Senon in the region of Clermont. The next day they
> repaired to Sainte Menehould. The Municipal Officers, who
> had been informed of their impending arrival by a letter from
> the two aeronauts, welcomed them at the gates of the town,
> accompanied by the Knights of the Arquebus in full armour.

They presented an honorary draught of wine to the two gentlemen and invited them to go down to the Town Hall where food and drink were awaiting them. They were led through a throng of cheering citizens to the Hall, where they dined.

The Magistrates of Lille, felicitating MM. Blanchard and l'Epinard on their aerial voyage when they went down into the town, a record of the event was entered in the registers. M. Blanchard had been granted the sum of 1,200 pounds French on his departure; they issued an order that he be granted a similar sum for his return, unless he prefer a box of gold decorated with the insignia of the town, of the same value and with a suitable inscription. As for the Chevalier de l'Epinard, the Magistrates reserved the right to offer him a gift.

Some years after this, an Englishman named Murray experimented with a parachute in Portsmouth, where he threw himself off a church tower and came down safely. Much encouraged, he tried the same thing from the Bell Tower of Chichester Cathedral, but about 14 feet from the top he was caught by a gust of wind, which blew him and his parachute alongside each other in mid-air. He managed to right himself but the wind caught him again. Murray fell to the ground, blood gushing from his ears, nose and mouth, and was unconscious for hours.

By the time Blanchard was ready to make his epic balloon trip across the Channel from Dover to Calais, in January 1795, he had abandoned carrying a parachute because of its weight and apparent uselessness. His companion was Dr John Jeffries, an American, who was acting as Blanchard's sponsor. Blanchard was resentful of Jeffries' presence, perhaps because he did not want to share the kudos that would go with triumph. He thought of several reasons why the American should stay on the ground, among the more convincing of which was that the balloon could not carry more than one person in addition to its ballast.

Blanchard was not above trickery to prove his point, even to the extent of loading his pockets with lead to increase his weight artificially. Even when he discovered this, Jeffries bore Blanchard no ill-will, but accompanied him as if nothing untoward had happened.

A combination of bad piloting and a probable leak in the balloon helped to justify fears for their safety. So unresponsive was the balloon in the early stages of its flight that ballast and every-thing else was eventually jettisoned in order to lighten the weight. By the time the pair had made landfall in the Forest of Guisnes, clothing, anchors, 'steering' gear, ornaments, oars, wings—even Jeffries' jacket and Blanchard's trousers—had been thrown overboard.

It was an undignified end to one era; another was about to begin.

2

TRIALS AND ERRORS

In 1793, it is reported, a French general named Bournonville was sent by the National Convention with four companions to begin negotiations with the Prince of Saxe-Coburg. Without warning, all five were seized and put in prison in the fortress of Olmutz. Bournonville, determined to escape, jumped with an umbrella from a window 40 feet up—a piece of daring that merely earned him a broken leg and another spell behind bars.

Whether this story is true or not, the hesitant early steps with umbrellas, parachutes and the use of animals as cargo, soon lengthened into strides, thanks largely to another Frenchman, André-Jacques Garnerin. He registered his achievement with history above what is today the Parc de Monceau in Paris, becoming the first human being to drop from a balloon and land alive.

Garnerin's first balloon ascent had been in 1787 from Metz. But the French Revolution, in which he fought, checked his aeronautical career in mid-flight, so to speak. He had been sent by his Government in 1793 as a Special Commissioner to the Army of the North, was taken prisoner and confined in a fortress in Buda, Hungary, for three years. Here, like General Bournonville, Citizen Garnerin began to toy with thoughts of escaping by parachute.

In the programme for his Paris descent of 1797, Garnerin explained:

The love of liberty so naturally gave rise to many projects to release myself from the rigorous detention. To surprise the vigilance of the sentries, force walls 10 feet thick, throw myself from the ramparts without being injured, were schemes that afforded recreation.

Blanchard's idea of presenting large surfaces to the air to

increase its resistance, and the known acceleration of movement in all falling bodies, appeared to me only to require a careful mathematical comparison to be employed with certain success. I applied myself to the problem. After deciding on the size of the parachute for descending from a rampart or a precipice, by natural sequence I devised the size and form of a parachute for a descent of several thousand feet by an aeronaut.

Garnerin's dream of escape from prison, hardly realistic in the circumstances, came to nought, but his resolve to make a parachute jump after his release was firm. His hopes were realised on October 22, 1797 with a parachute shaped like an umbrella, in 32 ribbed segments of white canvas and 23 feet in diameter when open. At the top there was a flat disc of wood, to which were hinged the parachute ribs, and four feet below this, a wooden hoop 8 feet in diameter from which hung the long skirt of the rest of the parachute. The whole assemblage was attached to the net of Garnerin's balloon by means of a central pole, like an umbrella handle, which poked into an aperture at the top. Garnerin was to travel in a basket underneath.

In common with all pioneers challenging the unknown, the Frenchman was not short of courage. He conducted his experiment, using himself as the willing guinea-pig, entirely alone; any credit for its success would belong to him, any blame for failure would attach—no doubt posthumously—to him too, for the parachute was made to his design.

As it happened, Garnerin's self-confidence was justified, but at times it was a close-run thing because the parachute oscillated so violently on its way down. A contemporary account, describing the scene in the Parc de Monceau, noted that a 'deep silence reigned in the assembly and anxiety showed on all faces. When he reached a height of 3,000 feet he cut the cords which held the parachute to the balloon . . . the latter exploded [sic] and the parachute began to descend with such rapidity that a cry of horror escaped from the spectators and several ladies fainted.'

Garnerin nevertheless reached the ground safely, mounted a

horse and rode back to the park and a 'stormy ovation'. Many years later, a noted compatriot, Charles Dollfus, founder of the Musée de l'Air in Paris and still one of the world's leading balloonists, was to describe it as '*un des grands actes d'héroisme de l'histoire humaine*'.

Garnerin's chronicler wrote of the 'rapidity' of the parachute's descent. Rapid it may have seemed at that time, but not today. At twenty-three feet flying diameter, Garnerin's parachute was a good deal bigger than, say, the RAF's emergency parachute used now, and his descent would have been considerably slower than a pilot's, though not as stable. One of Garnerin's problems was that after a drop he was invariably sick as a result of severe oscillation.

In aeronautics, as in other spheres, the progress of feminine emancipation during the nineteenth century brought to light a number of courageous, and often great, women. One such was Garnerin's own wife, Jeanne-Geneviève. Two years after his first jump, she enhanced her reputation as the world's first woman balloonist by becoming also the first woman to make a successful parachute descent. And some years later, Garnerin's niece Eliza was to make a considerable name for herself as a professional parachutist; between 1815 and 1836 she made nearly forty jumps.

Garnerin's fifth parachute descent was also the first ever to be made over England. Enjoying a brief respite in the war against Napoleon granted by the Peace of Amiens (only three years were to pass before Trafalgar) the English were, for once, well-disposed towards the French, particularly a man like Garnerin with outstanding personal qualities. So, on September 21, 1802, excited Londoners paid five shillings each to watch the spectacle, at St George's Parade in North Audley Street.

Interest was not confined to the Parade: one observer said it attracted the biggest crowd London had ever seen, with people filling the streets for miles around, as far afield as Temple Bar to the east and Primrose Hill to the north. Pot-boys from public houses nearby were kept busy climbing up with jugs of porter, pipes and tobacco for the spectators, who so crowded the specially erected scaffolding that there were fears for their safety. Sightseers anxious to miss nothing clambered up to every accessible vantage point to see the event, even sitting astride gabled house-tops and clinging to the chimney-stacks.

On this clear autumn evening only the merest south-westerly breeze stirred the treetops. By 5.15 p.m. Garnerin's huge striped balloon had been filled with hydrogen and the delicate process of attaching the parachute began. The sides of the cotton canopy, as it hung from the balloon, were about fifteen feet long, resembling, as women spectators were amused to note, a hooped petticoat. Under the parachute, the imperturbable Monsieur Garnerin fixed the basket, the cords from the parachute hem and those from the basket being gathered together in a firm knot above his head.

During these preparations some of the crowd became restive and over-eager. There was a good deal of jostling around the basket, which caused Garnerin and his assistant almost to lose patience with them. Eventually, all was ready and Garnerin, well-primed with porter, climbed in. The scene must have been deeply impressive, with crowds as far as the eye could see, and in the centre the balloon and parachute, together totalling 120 feet in height.

The shouting grew, the last rope was cut, and the mighty structure glided silently upwards, with Garnerin leaning from his basket and waving to the multitude with his silk tricolour. Here is Garnerin's own account:

I suspended my parachute to the balloon. This painful and difficult operation was executed with all possible address by the assistance of the most distinguished personages. The parachute was gradually suspended, and the breeze which was very gentle, did not produce the least obstacle. At length I hastened to ballast my bark, and to place myself in it: a sight which the public contemplated with deep interest—it seemed at that moment as if every heart beat in unison for, although I have not the advantage of speaking English, everyone understands my signs. I ascertained the height of the barometer, which was twenty-nine and a half inches. I now pressed the moment of my departure and the period of fulfilling my engagements with the British public.

All the cords were cut; I arose amidst the most impressive silence . . . and discovered from on high the countless multitude that sent up sighs and prayers for my safety. I quickened my ascending impulse and rose through light and thin vapours, where the cold air informed me that I was entering the upper region. . .

I examined my barometer, which I found had fallen to twenty-three inches. The sky was clear, the moment favourable, and I threw down my flag to show the people assembled that I was on the point of cutting the cord that suspended me between heaven and earth. I made every necessary disposition, prepared my ballast and measured with my eye the vast space that separated me from the rest of the human race. . .

I then took out my knife with a hand firm from a conscience void of reproach, and which had never been lifted against anyone but in the field of victory, I cut the cord. My balloon rose, and I felt myself precipitated with a velocity which was checked by the sudden unfolding of my parachute. I saw that all my calculations were just, and my mind remained calm and serene. I endeavoured to modulate my gravitation, and the oscillation which I experienced increased in proportion as I approached the breeze that blows in the middle regions: nearly ten minutes had elapsed, and I felt that the more time I took in descending the safer I should reach the ground.

At length I perceived thousands of people, some on horseback, others on foot, following me, all of whom encouraged me by their wishes, while they opened their arms to receive me.

I came near the earth, and after one bound, I landed and quitted the parachute without shock or accident. The first person who came to me pressed me in his arms; but without losing any time, I employed myself in detaching the principal circle of the parachute, anxious to save the instrument that had so well guaranteed me, but a crowd soon surrounded me—laid hold of me, and carried me in triumph, till an indisposition, the consequence and effect of the oscillation I had experienced, obliged me to stop.

I was then seized with a painful vomiting, which I usually experience for several hours after a descent in a parachute. The interval of a moment, however, permitting me to get on horseback, a numerous cavalcade approached to keep off the crowd, whose enthusiasm and transport incommoded me not a little. The Duke of York was amongst the horsemen, and the procession proceeded with great difficulty in the midst of the crowd, who shouted their applause, and had before the tricoloured flag which I had thrown down and which was carried by a Member of Parliament. . .

At length, after several incidents, all produced by the universal interest with which I was honoured, I withdrew from the crowd without any other accident than that of having my right foot jammed between the horse I rode and a horseman who pressed too close. . . . .

My parachute was preserved as well as could be expected, a few of the cords only were cut—it is now exhibited at the Panthéon, where a great concourse of persons have been to examine it.[1]

In the ten minutes that he was in the air, spectators in St George's Parade saw Garnerin almost disappear from view. In fact, he was above Tottenham Court Road when he cut himself and the parachute loose.

His account was not exaggerated. As the parachute lurched earthwards some way north of St Pancras Church, it was seen to sway so violently—far worse than in Paris five years before—that at times basket and parachute were almost alongside each other.

When he landed, he was certainly sick, as always, but he recovered sufficiently to dispense handshakes to applauding well-wishers, several of whom ran up to the parachute and tore strips of coloured paper off the basket for souvenirs. The Duke of York's presence at the descent was a nice piece of irony, for he it

[1] Translation from *The Annual Visitor*, 1803.

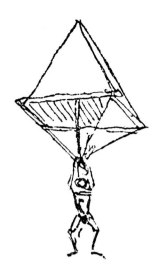

Leonardo da Vinci sketched a pyramid-shaped parachute (*above*) *circa* 1485, while an unknown contemporary of his was thinking along conical lines (*left*). Veranzio devised a sail-like version (*below left*) in 1595 ('Homo volans'), and William Newton in 1863 designed a balloon which in an emergency would descend on a parachute 'skirt' (*below right*).

(*Left*) The first parachute jump in Britain was made by a French balloonist, André-Jacques Garnerin, over London in 1802. Among the spectators was Robert Cocking, who was to jump to his death in 1837 from a saucer-shaped parachute (*above and below*) at the age of 61.

was who commanded the Austrian division which had taken Garnerin prisoner some years earlier.

If Garnerin was once again hero of the day, parachuting was certainly not. Several newspapers severely admonished the public for supporting the event and, also, by implication, Garnerin, for initiating it. *The Sun*, a London evening newspaper of the day, said:

> This is the first experiment of the kind in this Country, and we sincerely hope it will be the last. We mean not to detract from the skill and the courage displayed by M. Garnerin upon this occasion; indeed, it would be impossible if we were so inclined; but the man who could feel any pleasure in seeing the life of his fellow creature exposed to such imminent danger, without any adequate cause, must possess either the most unjustifiable curiosity, or the most brutal apathy.

Looking back on this 176 years later, one finds it easy to criticise this attitude, a fairly general one, as shortsighted. Though ballooning was about to enter its heyday, Cayley's development of true winged flight had hardly reached infancy, and the parachute's potentialities as a life-saving device could hardly have been foreseen. It had a long way to go before attaining complete efficiency in any case: Garnerin's experiences had proved that.

Among those who had watched Garnerin's momentous London jump was a 25-year-old water-colour painter and ballooning enthusiast, Robert Cocking. Disturbed and intrigued by the Frenchman's uncomfortable trip down, he resolved to succeed where Garnerin had partially failed.

Cocking spent years studying parachutes in an attempt to arrive at a stable design. At first he thought Garnerin's oscillation might be cured by providing an unlikely-sounding system of adjustable weights mounted to slide on rods. He then hit on the idea of an inverted cone, like a saucer—having observed, it is said, that a parasol which one day fell handle downwards from a balcony hit the ground with the stick uppermost. Another reason for choosing this strange shape could possibly have been that Sir George Cayley, known today as the father of aeronautics and the true inventor of the aeroplane, wrote an article in February 1810 (seven years after Garnerin's London descent) in which he condemned Garnerin's parachute as being 'nearly the worst possible'. In Cayley's view, based on his observations of the goat's-beard plant, the seeds of which are wafted away on small dihedral 'parachutes', the inverted cone shape was preferable.[1] It was to be many years, though, before Robert Cocking could put a modified version to the test.

After 1802, parachuting continued apace abroad. On July 24, 1808, a Polish balloonist, Jordski Kuparento, ascended from Warsaw in a balloon which caught fire and forced him to make the first life-saving jump with a parachute.

Within a few years, parachutes were being used, along with rockets, in war. In Britain, Colonel Congreve, in a book published for the information of officers of the Rocket Corps, included a description of a 42-pounder light ball or floating carcass rocket containing a parachute flare. The flare, capable of burning for ten minutes, had a range of $1\frac{3}{4}$ miles.

The first parachute jump made in America was by Louis-Charles Guillé who, in 1819 during a series of balloon exhibitions, made a parachute descent above Jersey City from a height of 500 feet.

That same year was one of tragedy for the Blanchard family in France, and a parachute was the indirect cause. Blanchard's wife Magdeleine, a noted woman balloonist, a solo professional of note and a rival of Garnerin's niece Eliza, was taking part in an exhibition balloon ascent involving fireworks at the Tivoli Gardens in Paris. Four hundred feet up, her balloon aglow with fizzing fire, she began to send down on little parachutes 'bombs' of silver rain. Suddenly, to the crowd's horror, the balloon caught fire and the envelope, ablaze, sank quickly to earth, throwing Mme Blanchard to her death among the rooftops of the Rue de Provence. The

---

[1] A model of Cayley's dihedral parachute, the only known surviving item of his aeronautical apparatus, is on display at the headquarters of the Royal Aeronautical Society. Cayley's notes of measurements, which he made when testing it, can be seen on its underside.

cause of the fire is thought to have been a down-draught of gas from the balloon's neck coming into contact with the wand she used to touch off the fireworks.

In England, references to parachutes appeared sporadically in the press. In May 1826, a reader of *Mechanics' Magazine*, signing himself 'Daedalus', suggested copying parachutes from nature, using as models the seeds of syngenesious plants carried through the air. His suggestion for the best form of parachute was 'that of a wheel, from the centre of which should be suspended a pole of adequate length... The spokes of this wheel should be made of the lightest materials, as of cane, and they should have an orbit of strong string, and interior circles of the same materials. Between them, large and strong feathers might be fixed in holes prepared to receive them in the cane . . . the whole would then form a machine resembling the winged down of plants.' Experiments, added 'Daedalus' prudently, should start on a small scale before man-sized ones were made.

For many years no parachute jumps were attempted at all in England. Certainly, Cocking was in no position to try. He was not commercially successful as a painter and had little money. He had to be content to experiment with models, dropping them from high points like the Monument and on Hampstead Heath, so that he could make comparisons with Garnerin's type. But for an opportunity to translate theory into fact Cocking had to wait thirty-five years.

His moment came in 1837, when he was sixty-one, with the advent of a great new balloon, made shortly before for the use of Charles Green, the most famous aeronaut of his day. In his field, Green was to be remembered for two developments along with his ballooning exploits: the introduction of coal gas in 1821 as a cheaper, if less buoyant, substitute for hydrogen, and the use of the trail-rope to drag along the ground and provide automatic ballast for low-level flights.

Green's new balloon, the Royal Vauxhall, was a huge and colourful affair fashioned out of more than 2,000 yards of crimson and white silk. In November 1836 the balloon and its pilot figured in a notable marathon trip. With two passengers—Robert Hollond M.P., sponsor of the flight, and Monck Mason, a leading authority on aeronautics, they rose from Vauxhall Gardens, glided over southern England, crossed the Channel and landed in a field near Weilberg in the Duchy of Nassau eighteen hours and 480 miles later—a distance record which remained unbroken until 1907.

Only a balloon of the stature and lifting power of the Royal Vauxhall (now re-named the Nassau) could carry the parachute which Cocking had designed. His parachute was not yet made, and lacking the resources to build it himself, he was forced to turn to others. But whom? After much thought, he went along to Vauxhall Gardens, near Millbank, London, a favourite ballooning venue whose proprietors also owned the Royal Nassau balloon. Cocking suggested they should finance the parachute, and he in return would provide what he fondly hoped would be a spectacular performance.

And so the parachute took shape—a huge saucer fashioned out of Irish linen, with ribs and braces, and 33 feet in diameter, with paintings decorating its underside. Framing the parachute at its widest was a metal hoop 107 feet 4 inches in circumference. The whole contrivance weighed 223 pounds—about ten times the weight of a modern parachute—added to which was Cocking's own weight of 170 pounds.

He could hardly have had a more capable balloonist than Green who, it might be thought, would be enthusiastic to help the elderly pioneer realise his life's ambition. Not at all; he was most unwilling. He was anxious on his own account about the risk involved in the great upward thrust of the balloon which would follow the release of the parachute and its 400 pounds load; and he feared for Cocking's safety because the parachute had not been tested using a dead weight. Eventually he refused to cut the parachute free, and insisted on the installation of a 'liberating iron' so that Cocking could release himself.

There were doubts about the strength of the tin tubing frame, which Cocking's friends felt would be stronger made of ash.

Cocking would have none of it; the whole design and execution, he maintained, had been approved by scientists and was therefore ideal, and posters advertising the descent made confident references to the 'unerring principles' on which Cocking's parachute was constructed.

Monck Mason was so pessimistic about Cocking's chances that at two o'clock in the morning of the day announced for the descent, July 24, 1837, he sent an absurdly verbose and gloom-laden letter to the *Morning Herald*. Too late for publication in full, it appeared only in severely truncated form, and the impact of its message, including this pertinent paragraph, was lost: 'I have no hesitation', he wrote, 'in predicting that one of two events must inevitably take place . . . either [the parachute] will come to the ground with a degree of force we have before shown to be incompatible with the final preservation of the individual, or should it be attempted to make it sufficiently light to resist this conclusion it must give way beneath the undue exercise of force which will necessarily develop in the descent. . .'

London's crowds, on the other hand, seemed to expect another Garnerin-like triumph. They thronged Vauxhall Gardens and the surrounding streets in their thousands. The day had dawned bright and clear, but in the way of English weather, by five in the afternoon the skies had clouded over. In the Gardens, the Nassau balloon grew bloated with gas. Once filled, it rose slightly to allow the strange dish of a parachute to be suspended underneath.

If Cocking was tense, he kept it well in check; not for a moment did he publicly countenance any possibility of failure, and he told observers so in forceful terms.

Into the balloon's car climbed the grimly hopeful Mr Green and his companion, Edward Spencer, while beneath them, in the parachute's wicker basket, stood the elderly Mr Cocking, a short stout figure in striped satin jacket and white trousers, waving cheerfully to the crowds. The band of the Surrey Yeomanry struck up the National Anthem, there was a round of cheering and clapping from the multitude, and the balloon drifted majestically upwards into a gentle north-west wind.

Almost immediately a complication arose. Two hundred feet up, the balloon lost the cloth tube carefully provided to jettison ballast away from the parachute's 'bowl', and the two men had to throw out portions of ballast as best they could. The balloon, the three men and the weird parachute cargo wafted slowly southeastwards. Cocking had hoped to release himself at 8,000 feet, but despite numerous discharges of ballast, the balloon could not gain sufficient height quickly enough.

'As soon as we had attained the height of 5,000 feet,' said Green later, 'I told him that it would be impossible for us to get up as high as he desired in sufficient time for him to descend by the light of day. Upon this, Mr Cocking said, "Then I shall very soon leave you; but tell me whereabouts I am." Mr Spencer answered, "We appear to be on a level with Greenwich." I then asked him if he felt himself quite comfortable, and whether he found that the practical trial bore out the calculations he had made. Mr Cocking replied, "Yes, I never felt more comfortable or more delighted in my life." Shortly afterwards, Mr Cocking said, "Well, now I think I shall leave you." I answered, "I wish you a very good night and a safe descent, if you are determined to make it, and not to use the tackle." '

The 'tackle' was some apparatus rigged up by the manager of the Vauxhall Gardens and Green to help Cocking up into the balloon basket if he changed his mind about the jump. Cocking ignored the final chance to withdraw and said simply, 'Goodnight, Spencer; goodnight, Green', and tugged at the liberating mechanism. The first attempt failed, then with a powerful jerk, Cocking released it.

Immediately, according to Green, the balloon, freed of its burden at last, 'shot upwards with the velocity of a sky-rocket'.

'The effect upon us at this moment is almost beyond description. The immense machine which suspended us between heaven and earth, whilst it appeared to be forced upwards with terrific violence and rapidity through unknown and untravelled regions, amidst the howlings of a fearful hurricane, rolled about as though revelling in a freedom for which it had long struggled. . . Gas was rushing in torrents from the upper and lower valves. . . . Had it not been for the application to our mouths of two pipes leading into an air bag with which we had furnished ourselves previously to starting, we must within a minute have been suffocated, and so, but by different means, have shared the melancholy fate of our friend.'

For hardly had poor Cocking cut himself free of the balloon when the fears of so many sceptics became justified. To the accompaniment of crackling wood and crumpling tin, the parachute canopy and its framework collapsed, and Cocking plummeted to earth with the swaying mass of debris miles from the crowds who had cheered him on his way. He was found among the wreckage of his beloved parachute on Burnt Ash Hill, near Lee Green, Kent, not quite dead but so badly injured that he died within minutes.

There was a macabre sequel to this tragedy. Shortly after he fell, Cocking's body, along with the remains of the parachute, were taken to the Tiger's Head public house nearby. There, on the floor, they were exhibited to the public in a degrading peep-show, the body and the parachute each at sixpence a time, tickets being provided in the bar. Only after protestations from Mr Gye, manager of Vauxhall Gardens, was the sordid little exhibition stopped.

Today, Robert Cocking's grave can still be seen in the churchyard at Lee—a sad memorial to a stubborn, persistent, foolish but heroic old man.

Need Cocking have died? What went wrong? A month after his death, Mrs George Graham, the wife of a balloonist and one herself, took part at Hackney in a benefit exhibition in aid of Cocking's widow. She ascended in the Royal Victoria balloon, and from the basket dropped two model parachutes, one of the Garnerin type and one like Cocking's. It was Cocking's which made the better descent.

The American aeronaut John Wise, who was in his third year of parachuting, was also curious at Cocking's death. Three months after the tragedy he compared Cocking's inverted cone with the orthodox umbrella type of Garnerin. Wise took his balloon up at

Philadelphia bearing a couple of test 'chutes and released them at 2,500 feet, his dog Tray in the basket of the Garnerin and his cat Tabitha borne by the Cocking. The first oscillated wildly like its full-sized predecessor, but the Cocking version came down safely, if rotating slightly.

It seems strange that if Cocking's parachute emerged as the more stable of the two, that his should fail so fatally in fact. It is, of course, not certain that a true comparison was being made.

In a fascinating paper considering Garnerin's and Cocking's parachute designs, published in the Royal Aeronautical Society's Journal in 1964, S. B. Jackson, then chief designer of Irvin Air Chute of Great Britain, makers of the parachute which became standard for the RAF in the 1920s, considered this problem. Garnerin's parachute fabric, he pointed out, was completely impervious to air which, coupled with the flattish shape of the canopy, would not be inclined to give good stability. At that time, he observes, there was 'almost a complete failure to comprehend the problem'.

This was also the case with the contemporary commentators on the Cocking tragedy, says Jackson. 'It is almost certain . . . that Cocking's parachute failed for purely structural reasons', and although a number of parachute designs that were supposed to give good stability and yet not suffer from structural weakness were considered soon afterwards, none was tried out and the conventional parachute continued to be the one mostly used.

A year after Cocking's death, John Poole, a popular author of the day, wrote a book called *Crotchets in the Air*, a descriptive piece on a balloon trip with Charles Green. He wrote, *inter alia*: 'We all know the fate of that poor simpleton, Cocking; so much for parachutes! . . . but I entertain serious doubts as to whether parachutes, or even firework ascents can be rendered serviceable to science in any of its branches—unless coffin-making be reckoned of their number.'

No prophet was Poole, but there is no doubt that he had caught the nation's mood.

3

TRIUMPHS AND TRAGEDIES

SUCH WAS the wave of indignation following Cocking's death that it seemed only the most fanatical or vainglorious of adventurers would risk public opprobrium by making similar attempts. In the pages of the specialist journals, thought was given to remedy rather than remonstration. The noted innovator, Colonel Francis Maceroni, who in his time designed an armoured ship, paddlewheel and steam coach, wrote three weeks after the Cocking disaster saying he had experimented with weights and felt that, unlike Cocking's, 'the proper and perfectly efficacious construction for a parachute is similar to an umbrella; only, instead of whalebones or canes being brought to a point and attached to a stick, they must be attached to a ring or hoop of wood, of a diameter equal to one-fifth or one-quarter of the diameter of the parachute. Thus, there will be a large hole in the centre of the machine, through which compressed and accumulated air will rush and infallibly prevent its overturning, or even oscillating, at all.'

In 1804, according to the colonel, a man was seen by thousands to leap off the bridge of La Tenità, which connected two streets by passing over another street, 122 feet below. He himself had seen the man shortly afterwards. Fastened to his waist was an ordinary umbrella, but larger, and he reached the ground uninjured. This jumper had taken the precaution of fixing stays all round the stick. Colonel Maceroni fallaciously claimed that Garnerin's parachute had oscillated only because the hole in the centre was no larger than the crown of a man's hat.

An architectural draughtsman, George Mackenzie, suggested a parachute equipped with a weight at the bottom of the rigging lines where the parachutist would normally be. The jumper would sit under the crown of the parachute, where there would be a ring-shaped tube, several feet wide, containing air.

Fifteen months after Robert Cocking's death, John Hampton, aged thirty-nine, an erstwhile sailor who had become a professional balloonist, chose to ignore popular sentiment and the criticism of his friends by making a parachute jump. Unlike Cocking, Hampton wanted to play safe with a parachute of orthodox design, modelled on Garnerin's of thirty-six years before. There was one difference: Garnerin's model unfolded after release from his balloon, while Hampton's was designed to have already opened out, like Cocking's. The canopy was scalloped at the hem, made of stout gingham and measured 21 feet in diameter when fully expanded on its 8-foot ribs of whalebone. Sticks of bamboo connected the canopy to a hollow brass tube 11 feet long, through which ran a rod with a wicker basket on the lower end.

A few days before the jump took place, Hampton ran into trouble. It had dawned on the owners of Montpellier Gardens, Cheltenham, where the descent was scheduled for October 3, 1838, that if the venture failed, no small blame would fall on them for sanctioning it. Mr Spinney, the manager of the gas works which had contracted to fill Hampton's balloon, turned for guidance to the local magistrates. Their worships, while admitting they had no legal powers to interfere with the project, sympathised with the protesters and suggested that if Mr Spinney refused to supply the balloonist with gas, a parachute jump would be legally prevented.

Hampton argued hard, and was eventually allowed to have his gas on two conditions: that the ascent must be a captive one, and that any parachute jump must be made within the Gardens. Reluctantly, Hampton went through the motions of keeping his part of the bargain, aware no doubt that half a jump was better than none at all.

But he was not the sort to be easily deterred. When the day came, the balloon was inflated, the parachute attached beneath it, a large coil of strong rope hitched to the parachute basket and the long end grasped firmly by twenty workmen who had been instructed to hold fast at all costs. When the balloon and parachute were about forty feet above the ground, Hampton, who had been secretly abetted by his friend Granville Fletcher, produced a knife and quickly cut the tether. The balloon rose till it reached 8,000 feet (1,000 feet higher than he had originally planned). Once more his knife went to work, this time to separate the parachute.

'My balloon ascended from me immediately after the separation, for some hundred feet,' reported Hampton later, 'and with a terrific noise rushed through the atmosphere, and in the space of a few seconds only, burst over my head with the violence of a thunderbolt.'

Determined as he was to succeed, Hampton had not been wholly confident. During his balloon ascent he was seen to wave, not the customary Union Jack but, his audience were astonished to see, a tricolour—the very one flourished by Garnerin in 1802. Three days later came the reason for this eccentric gesture. 'It might be inquired why he did not rise under the standard of England,' wrote a fellow member of the Ancient Order of Druids in the *Cheltenham Free Press*. 'He would answer—though morally certain of success, an accident *might* occur, he *might* fail, and as an Englishman he was determined that in no event connected with him should an enterprise under the auspices of the British flag be sullied by defeat.'

Hampton did not fail. His descent was peacefully undisturbed by any dangerous oscillation, though on landing he did hit his head on an iron hoop used to strengthen the wicker basket, and cut himself above one eye. But the important thing for Hampton, as he climbed out of his parachute 12 minutes 40 seconds after release, was that he had secured his place in the annals of aeronautics as the first Englishman to make a parachute jump and live.

Hampton, an aeronautical showman typical of his time, was compelled to pander to some of the worst elements of the London crowds, many of whom preferred spills laced with their thrills. The following year he planned to ascend again, this time from

Cremorne Gardens, Chelsea, with the object of making another jump.

Advance publicity for balloonists could never be accused of excessive modesty, as the wording on the poster shows:

MR HAMPTON, the unrivalled and intrepid Aeronaut, will have the honour to make his first appearance this Season at the above Splendid and Highly Distinguished Grounds, on Thursday, June 13th, 1839, being his 15th Ascent with his Magnificent Balloon, the 'Albion', and at an Altitude of at least 10,000 feet from the Earth separate himself and Apparatus from the Balloon and descend in his Royal Safety Parachute. This truly enterprising and unparalleled feat having been successfully performed by Mr Hampton last autumn, at Cheltenham, in the presence of an immense Assemblage of Rank and Fashion, including upwards of 100,000 Spectators!!!

It was something of an anti-climax when Thursday, June 13 turned out to be dangerously windy. Considering the prospects in Cremorne Gardens, Hampton knew as he glanced round the great crowds pouring in, that he could never clear the nearby trees. He decided to call off the ascent. The crowds thereupon demanded their money back, and Hampton tried to persuade them to come back next day. They would have none of it, and Hampton reluctantly released the balloon and went through with the parachute jump. The parachute descended at a 'frightful speed', according to witnesses, and when a horseman galloped off to look for Hampton he found him at Walham Green, having injured himself by landing against a wall. The cords on his parachute had become tangled, hampering control.

The Press of the day was still disdainful of the lower orders who sought their pleasure in other people's risks. 'The bravery, or temerity, of Mr Hampton, may perhaps excite admiration in some breasts, and in many, pity,' wrote one reporter, 'but the cold-blooded inhumanity of the brawling sightseers cannot otherwise be regarded than with a unanimous feeling of detestation.'

As a professional exhibitionist Hampton was a first-class salesman for himself and his skill as a performer, but he was also given
to a salesman's exaggeration. For example, he grossly overstated
the dangers of parachuting by saying that drops through the air
made breathing difficult. This was simply not true, and the effect
was to discourage experimentation with any parachute without a
rigid framework; a loose-canopied one would, it was thought,
produce a fall so rapid as to induce unconsciousness, a complete
misconception that was to persist at least for another eighty years.
It was the heyday of the showman rather than the experimenter. Along with concerts, theatrical firework displays, circus
turns, pony racing, gymnastics, singing and dancing, or simply
taking tea in the company of friends, balloon ascents and the
occasional parachute jump became accepted features of London's
outdoor entertainment. Aeronautic feats became increasingly
exotic to match the crowds' greedy appetite for novelty and
excitement. Charles Green, the famous balloonist who figured in
the Cocking incident and was a serious pioneer, was at one stage
reduced to ascending in his balloon on horseback. On another
occasion he took up a lady and a leopard as passengers.

To Green, in 1850, goes the credit of devising the first parachute
supply-dropping system. This was in an effort to save Sir John
Franklin, who had disappeared in the Arctic in 1847. Green made
a balloon of about 30 cubic foot capacity and capable of drifting
up to 600 miles, under which he attached packets and parachutes
for carrying food and messages. The intention was to release them
automatically by means of a slow-burning match.

Whether the drop was actually made or not is unknown. If it
was it was ineffective, for the bodies of Franklin and his colleagues
were found twelve years after they had disappeared.

A new kind of parachute contraption made its début in London
in June 1854, when Henri Letur, a diminutive 48-year-old Frenchman, brought over his 'parachute'—a large umbrella-shaped
canopy beneath which were wings which flapped 50 times a
minute by operating a treadle. Letur had made about 30 accident-
free trips with it in France, three of them over the Champs

Elysées before the Emperor and Empress. Letur could not take off from the ground unaided, but he could make a regulated, and safe, descent.

His first attempt in London, from Cremorne Gardens, took him to Blackheath, where he literally dropped in to see some friends after a descent which lasted three-quarters of an hour. His second, on June 27, was beneath W. H. Adams' balloon, and was fatal.

The Frenchman, a slightly deformed figure prematurely aged by years of circus injuries, had laughed off spectators' pessimism, and certainly the lift-off was smooth enough. But as balloon and jumper swung away to the north-east, Adams realised above Camden Town that one of the supporting ropes to Letur's device was twisted. Being unable to speak French, he could not warn Letur, who in turn could not understand English. Over open country at Tottenham, he cut two of the three ropes, leaving the third still entangled with one of the wings. Adams put the balloon down slowly, but the wind caught it and blew it across the field and through trees with considerable violence. Poor Letur was seriously injured and, with blood pouring down his face, lay where he fell, moaning simply, 'Mon dieu, mon dieu' until he was taken to hospital, where he died eight days later.

At his inquest, several jurors called for a letter to be sent to the Secretary of State urging that similar parachute descents should be banned. The majority, however, felt that this would only obstruct the progress of science.

The antics of some performers in the aeronautic 'circus' around this time incurred the outspoken disapproval, possibly inspired by professional jealousy, of John Hampton, and he told them so in print. In particular, he seized upon two French aeronauts, Monsieur and Madame Poitevin, who had made numerous balloon ascents with animals. In the *Morning Herald* on September 6, 1852, Hampton attacked first their 'brutal system' of animal ascents, which he described as 'torture . . . with impunity'.

Then his anger turned upon Monsieur Poitevin alone. 'Now this bold and courageous husband', wrote Hampton acidly, 'intends to place his wife in the car of the parachute and for the gratification of vulgar taste, separate her from the balloon when at a great height.' He called on magistrates to stop the Frenchman's 'shameful propensities' and suggested that Monsieur Poitevin himself should make a jump—as Hampton himself had done fourteen years before.

This had no effect whatever on the French pair. Madame Poitevin went up from Cremorne Gardens attached to her husband's balloon 'Zodiac' and jumped with her parachute 'Meteor' in perfect style from 5,000 feet and landed amid tremendous applause.

The one-sided quarrel caught the eye of Sir George Cayley, an aeronautical genius who saw it as an opportunity for reiterating his ideas for so-called 'governable parachutes'.

Cayley was a fascinating man whose work has cast a long and beneficent shadow. But he was grossly underrated in his day: his name never appeared in the *Dictionary of National Biography*, and yet Charles Gibbs-Smith, the eminent aeronautical historian, has written, 'he is now seen to be the true inventor of the modern aeroplane—in the basic sense—and the founder of the science of aerodynamics applied to aircraft'. To Sir George he attributes no fewer than twenty-eight aeronautical 'firsts'. In other fields, too, he found outlets for his fertile imagination; as inventor of the caterpillar tractor and a type of artificial mechanical limb.

'As the subject of parachutes again attracts public attention', wrote Cayley to *Mechanics' Magazine* following the Hampton letter, 'permit me to suggest what would be an interesting addition to the mere hackneyed fact of their descent—their steerage from the moment they are liberated from the balloon to any desired landing-place, within about five to six times the distance horizontally that the balloon is then above the earth. . .'

Cayley then went on to describe, with sketches, his plan for a navigable parachute. He envisaged a large wing with a dihedral angle stretched on a framework and shaped vaguely like a fish, with a car suspended underneath. The whole structure, which was to be launched from a balloon, was in fact a glider. Cayley, now seventy-nine, must have been bitterly disappointed that nobody considered his idea worth pursuing.

As in other fields, the Victorians were richly fecund in ideas. Even if practice did not always, or even often, accord with theory, at least their optimism was impressive. Hugh Bell, a Londoner, patented in 1848 a sausage-shaped airship 56 feet long, with propellers to be worked by hand and a steering rudder behind. The balloon part was enclosed in flat silk bands for strength, and a single flat band fixed round its middle helped to convert it into a parachute in case of accident. Accompanying this was a device called a water grapnel which could be dropped from a balloon into the sea; working on the same principle as the parachute, its collapsible 'umbrella' would unfold to act as a brake. Bell arranged trials in Vauxhall Gardens for his air vessel, but they were not successful.

With his silk bands idea, Bell may have been trying to reinforce a natural tendency for a rent balloon to form a parachute in any case. An impressive example of this occurred the previous year when four men endured one of the most frightening descents of all time. One of the Vauxhall balloons, Gypson's, was to make a night flight carrying 60 pounds of fireworks, to be set off as part of a late-night entertainment over the Gardens. Youngest in the crew was Henry Coxwell, who later became a prominent aeronaut.

The summer afternoon had been calm and hot, with prospects of a fine evening. Soon, however, clouds piled up, thunder rumbled in the distance and flashes of lightning lit up the London sky. After a hasty consultation among themselves the four decided that if the ascent were quick they could get up and get down safely before the storm was upon them.

So the balloon rose, with young Coxwell sitting on the hoop, ready to operate the valves. Minutes later the balloonists were thrilling the crowds with lavish festoons of Roman candles, petards and gold and silver rains. But four thousand feet up they found themselves in the middle of the storm. The balloon, lightened of its fireworks, was rising fast. Coxwell sensed imminent danger, and said so, but he was ignored. 'If the valve is not opened the balloon will burst!' warned Coxwell.

Almost as he spoke, lightning flashed to reveal a 16-foot gash in the balloon's envelope. With great presence of mind, Coxwell immediately cut the cord fastening the neck to the hoop of the fast-sinking balloon and, to their relief, the fabric leapt upwards to the limits of the net and spread out like a parachute, checking their fall. They came down, shaken but unharmed, in Pimlico.

The American balloonist John Wise had already carried out experiments along these lines in 1838. The first took place above Easton, Pennsylvania, on August 11. He intended to explode his balloon deliberately, but was forestalled—it did so by accident! The experiment worked, though; the lower part of the envelope was forced up into the net. His second experiment went wrong, because the envelope was forced sideways instead of upwards. He came down heavily but unhurt.

Although many decades were to pass before the virtues of, and the need for, an efficient parachute became clear, suggestions for improvements to the existing framed parachute were not lacking. Back to nature was the message of Mr William Bland of Hartlip, Kent, who after a Hampton parachute display wrote to *Mechanics' Magazine* maintaining that the parachute principle, as currently employed, was all wrong. And he sent the editor a box containing several 'most perfect and beautiful parachutes', actually the seeds, which resemble flue-brushes, of a plant called stag's horn. Another correspondent urged modelling the parachute on the convolvulus flower which, he had observed, when thrown into the air always fell stalk first.

It was the day of bizarre inventions, as complex as they were improbable. Most of them were doomed to be earthbound. John Henry Johnson, of Lincoln's Inn Fields, invented an elongated balloon with a platform suspended from it for aeronauts and machinery. There were to be steam-driven paddle wheels 'for the purpose of counteracting the action of the air against the balloon', and parachute- or umbrella-shaped propellers sliding back and forth on horizontal rods, pushing the air back behind them and propelling the device along, guided by horizontal sails, vertical sails and a rudder.

Another dreamer, Prosper Dartiguenave, chose a system of steam-driven parachutes for his contraption but this time vertically, and 'when the desired elevation has been attained, I direct my machine by means of a horizontal flapper. . . My machine is also provided with wings, the better to enable it to turn and which can have their direction changed at the will of the aeronaut.' Perhaps fortunately for the inventor, notice to proceed with letters patent was not given within the prescribed time limit.

One of the most eccentric of innovators was the Earl of Aldborough, who in 1855 patented a series of 'improvements' to aerial navigation. Page after page of the lengthy specification set out in astonishing detail an elaborate system of using aerostats, many based on the parachute, for use in war. The detailed drawings, which resembled quaintly made paper darts, were so vague, however, that it was difficult to imagine exactly what the noble earl was striving for.

He drew up plans, many times amended in subsequent years, for fortified ports, landing places or harbours for his warlike aerial vessels. A few years later, another hopeful inventor patented a balloon with flapping wings, based on the flap-valve principle, with valves that opened on the upstroke and closed on the down, with the object of obtaining lift. The wings, when stilled, would be used like a parachute to make the descent, as he put it, 'quite free from danger'.

The Montgolfier hot-air balloon was the subject of a provisional patient by a civil engineer, William Newton, in 1863. One of his modifications, applicable also to a gas-filled balloon, was a parachute round the balloon's 'waist'. The following year, the French aeronaut Eugène Godard built a huge balloon called 'L'Aigle', also a Montgolfière, which made two ascents from Cremorne Gardens, Chelsea. The eagle motif was painted large on the side, and above its waist, about a third of the way from the top, there was a segmented cloth parachute, looking like a circular wing, or absurdly ill-fitting tutu.

Ten years later, Albert Fleury came up with a strange variation on the parachute theme. If you attached a weight to the corners of a rectangular plate with cords of equal length, reasoned Fleury, it would drop vertically; but if the cords were unequal, it would descend on an incline.

In the same year, 1874, Vincent de Groof, a Belgian shoemaker, tried his hand at a flying machine that was a marriage (though not, as it turned out, a happy one) between wings and a parachute. De Groof had used his device with poor results in Belgium; now he came to London to try his luck. Before the Cremorne Gardens crowds on June 29, he fixed his apparatus under the 'Czar' balloon, piloted by Mr Simmons. The balloon rose and, the crowd was disappointed to see, swung away into Essex, and the landing that De Groof claimed took place well beyond view.

Doubts were expressed as to whether De Groof had actually cut free at all, so a few days later he was prevailed upon to repeat the performance, so that all could see him. This time there were no doubts. 'I must cut you loose,' shouted Simmons. 'Yes,' replied De Groof, 'and I can fall in the churchyard.' As soon as the rope was cut, the machine collapsed and sent its owner thudding to earth in the street. He died in Chelsea Infirmary.

A new device, a hybrid parachute-cum-kite, was produced in 1875 by Joseph Simmons (whether he was the balloonist or another of the family is not known). It was designed in fabric strengthened by a net and stretched on a framework, the whole 'parakite' resembling a piece of half-finished abstract paper sculpture. The kite, intended to carry an aeronaut in a car underneath, would be taken up by the wind and drop like a parachute. The army showed interest, but demonstrations at Chatham the following year proved disappointing; one machine was damaged before or during the flight, and the other crashed—an inauspicious start to the parakite's career which also spelt its finish.

4

ON WITH THE SHOWS

FOR MUCH of the nineteenth century, the parachute underwent little development. Its prime function was as an entertainment device to add drama to the flagging appeal of the simple balloon ascent. It was never seriously considered by aeronauts as a means of escape, for it was little use in stormy or windy weather, the sort of conditions which would call it into service. And the stiff-ribbed umbrella-type parachute could hardly be tucked away and forgotten until it was needed.

James Glaisher, a founder of the (Royal) Aeronautical Society in 1866, seemed to think the parachute might have a future, if not an immediate one. Writing on aeronautics in the ninth edition of the *Encyclopedia Britannica*, published in 1875, he said: 'Though we shall notice any particularly remarkable [balloon] ascents, we shall chiefly for the sake of describing the few that have been undertaken for the sake of advancing science, and which also are of permanent value. It will be necessary to make one exception to the rule, however, in the case of the parachute, the experiments with which require some notice, although they have been put to no useful purpose.'

Yet ballooning show-business was not without scientific value, and in 1880 a new milestone was reached in parachute history. The precursor of the modern parachute was invented—a flexible, unribbed version that would be filled out by the pressure of the air itself. It was not long before cotton gave way to the stronger and less bulky silk, but the parachute of the late nineteenth century was still attached to the balloon or basket by a cord, which had to be cut before descent. Free-fall ripcord parachutes were still years away.

The honour for inventing the flexible parachute falls to one of two men: either to Captain Tom Baldwin, an American, or to

Captain P. A. Van Tassell, a Dutchman who had settled in America. Though there is doubt concerning the true originator, historians believe the evidence tips the scales slightly in favour of Van Tassell, though Baldwin has received much of the credit. The new parachute was first tried out in a cattle field outside Los Angeles in the early 1880s. It was dropped from a hot-air balloon in preference to a gas-filled one because it could be reclaimed when the air cooled. (The expensive gas balloon was often lost.)

Surrounding Van Tassell were all the show-business trappings that characterised commercial jumps in those days, yet behind the ballyhoo there were undeniable risks: for example, the Dutchman weighed 200 pounds, and the parachute had not even been tested.

The canopy itself was unimpressive: it was not shaped, like the modern parachute, but lay on the ground as a flat disc. The cords from the canopy were tied to a trapeze fifteen feet below, the whole parachute being hung from the balloon's circumference.

Van Tassell ascended 4,000 feet, climbed from the balloon basket on to the trapeze and for a few seconds hung in space. Then he cut the parachute's umbilical cord and dropped. The canopy swelled out almost immediately, the shroud-lines tautened, and he touched down. Another showman's stunt had been completed, and another piece of pioneering triumphantly accomplished.

The name of Van Tassell's principal competitor, Captain Tom Baldwin, was remembered when the Dutchman's had almost melted into obscurity. Possibly the American was better at projecting his extrovert personality. Certainly he made an impression on the Prince of Wales, later Edward VII, for Baldwin was summoned to give a private command parachute-jumping performance before the Royal Family.

Baldwin's parachute differed little from that of Van Tassell, from whom, it was alleged, he had purloined the design. If he did, it was a prize piece of ingratitude, for the Dutchman had tutored Baldwin with all the parachuting knowledge and expertise he possessed. So the pair went their separate ways, touring the world—England, India, Turkey, Japan—in unfriendly rivalry, each with his own following of young daredevil disciples upon whom would descend the cloak of stardom when they had dropped for the last time.

The rewards could be highly lucrative. One of Baldwin's jumps was in 1885 at the Golden Gate Park, San Francisco, where he offered to jump for a dollar a foot of altitude. He made 1,000 dollars in one afternoon. Specialities were developed. A Baldwin pupil, Mark Berg, created a sensation by supporting himself beneath a parachute trapeze with his teeth gripping a leather strap. This stunt proved literally to be his downfall, for one day he bit right through the leather and dropped 4,000 feet to his death over Santa Monica.

Balloonists still worked to perfect ways of converting their balloons into parachutes in emergencies. Captain William Dale, an Englishman, conceived the idea of a central tube up through the balloon, this housing a cord connected to a layer of oiled silk at the top. Emergency action was to tug the cord and remove the oiled silk, and allow the balloon's envelope to surge up into the net in customary fashion, but fully under control because the lower valve could rise up the centre tube till it reached the top and keep the 'canopy' stable as it went.

Dale was killed when his balloon burst at Crystal Palace in 1892 —without his device to save him. This period was marked by a number of other accidents. One day in August 1891, 'Professor' George Higgins was taking part in a double parachute descent with his wife at a Leeds charity display. There was a dangerously high wind blowing, and Higgins' wife had just taken her seat on the trapeze, when Higgins joined her. Suddenly, seeing a two-foot tear develop in the balloon's envelope, officials leapt forward and hauled Mrs Higgins clear of the bar. Her husband, unaware of the damage to the balloon, shouted 'Let go!' and in the confusion was whisked skywards on the crossbar. A gust of wind carried the balloon against some telegraph wires and Higgins was swept off the bar, hurtling down backwards to his death on a barrier below.

A 23-year-old woman parachutist, Miss Maud Brooks, of Liverpool, was crippled for life during a Whitsun charity jump in

Dublin. She jumped from a balloon, but her parachute failed to open until only a few yards from the ground. The local paper, *Freeman's Mail*, commented bitterly: 'We have not conquered the beast in our nature when the element of danger in a parachutist descending from an altitude of 3,000 feet can attract thousands of eager spectators. The evil is aggravated, if anything, when the performer is a woman.'

A French aeronaut, Louis Capazza, invented a 'safety parachute' for a balloon in 1892. It resembled a closely-fitting egg cosy and the idea was that if the balloon burst, as Dale's did, the gas would be pushed out into the parachute above and through a chimney in the apex. Capazza tested this successfully in Paris at 3,700 feet when, using a grapnel, he deliberately and daringly ripped his balloon, 'Le Caliban', from top to bottom.

Two months later he brought 'Le Caliban' to England and quickly fell foul of the English crowds at a demonstration at the Welsh Harp, Hendon. During preparations for the ascent, there was confusion among his assistants, and the parachute 'hat' got twisted awry. In the melée the balloon went up, but without the parachute, which added to the chaos by fluttering down like a cloak over the struggling 'ground crew' below.

'Give us back our bobs!' came angry cries from the 6,000 spectators deprived of a show, and after a promise of another performance the following week, a crestfallen Monsieur Capazza was hustled into a hansom and escorted away by police. But the second performance was never given. Capazza was too disgusted at the crowd's behaviour.

Several useful new parachute designs emerged, including one in 1888 by an Italian, Guillermo Antonio Farini, and Baldwin, the American—a flexible, mushroom-shaped silk parachute without ribs and with a hole in the top. Thus the revival of the erroneous belief that a vent in the apex of a parachute helps to relieve air pressure and reduces oscillation. This may have been the result of diligent research by Baldwin; on the other hand there is something attractive about the story that the idea came to him from a boy bystander who had been watching a particularly unstable drop by

Baldwin in his flexible parachute. 'Mister,' said the boy, 'why don't you put a hole in the top?'

Baldwin's subsequent tests seemed to confirm his theory. Here then was a usable collapsible parachute capable of being carried by a moving aircraft, and anticipating the arrival of the Wright brothers and sustained powered flight by about fifteen years.

The design was welcomed, but not by everyone. Not, for example, by Thomas Moy, an engineer and patent agent who had invented and built a model steam-driven tandem-wing monoplane and tested it on a circular track at Crystal Palace in 1875. He was contemptuous of the Farini-Baldwin parachute and accused them of pandering to the multitudes for money with something that could have been predicted by a schoolboy. 'So far as science is concerned', wrote Moy in the *Mechanics' Magazine* in 1890, 'they have done literally nothing.'

Curiously blind to the possibilities of parachute escape from a heavier-than-air machine such as he himself had been trying to perfect, Moy scoffed at Baldwin's claim that he could 'steer' his canopy, and urged looking at nature for steerable parachutes, in particular the squirrel. 'The flying squirrel is a living parachute. . . When he starts from one tree to a lower branch on another, he does not miss his aim. Wind is allowed for, and he lands on the very spot he aimed at. Baldwin could not do that. But then the flying squirrel is not provided with an umbrella-top to do the trick with. He has extended aeroplanes.'

Moy said the squirrel would come a cropper if it tried to fall vertically. 'But it is too wise for that; it starts with initial velocity in a horizontal direction and so comes down very gently. . .' The 'wretched, unscientific gas-bag, and the pretty umbrella cover', added Moy scornfully, were ancient history.

Aerostats—primitive airships based on the balloon principle— were often designed now with some kind of built-in parachute device for emergencies. Sometimes it was nothing more than a surmounting canopy; in one case, the blades of fans provided to give lift to the aerostat were designed to flatten and close up to form a kind of parachute.

A German, Ludwig Rohrmann, found a new use for the parachute. He invented a parachute-carrying rocket for surveying or reconnaissance, the parachute dropping with a camera for taking bird's-eye-view observation shots.

In the United States, some inventors saw in parachutes the means of escaping from burning buildings, thus echoing the demonstration jump by the French physician Lenormand in 1783. One American inventor, Benjamin B. Oppenheimer, of Tennessee, made the incredible claim in 1879 that his 'New and Improved Fire Escape' would enable jumpers to leap from a blazing building of any height and land without injury on the ground.

Scepticism could be forgiven, since Mr Oppenheimer's parachute was only four or five feet in diameter and harnessed to the wearer's head! Despite the padded overshoes proposed, one feels that this inventor's device would have achieved only one result: the possibility of death by fire would have been replaced with certain death by parachute.

A rudimentary and highly hazardous forerunner of the ejection seat appeared in American balloons: a case divided into two compartments, one containing black powder and the other a parachute jumper. When the required height was reached, the case was thrown out, the parachutist lit the powder, a trap-door opened and out burst the jumper, parachute billowing, amid clouds of smoke. This attempt to enliven balloon jumping was abused, almost inevitably. One stunter substituted dynamite for the powder and succeeded in blasting himself to eternity and everything else rapidly to earth. In another case a trap-door jammed and the parachutist was stifled and burnt to death.

5

FLIGHT INTO DANGER

On December 17, 1903, from the sandy coast of North Carolina, two brothers excitedly sent home a telegraph to their father. It informed him that Orville and Wilbur Wright had become the first men ever to achieve sustained flight with a powered aircraft. For that morning the 'Flyer', their 12 horse-power 40-foot wingspan biplane, had made four flights, the shortest of 12 seconds, the longest of 59. Man was airborne at last.

But although he had conquered the air, he was not yet master of his fate. He was as strong—or as vulnerable—as the flimsy machine which bore him. Little real thought was devoted to the question of escape; the overwhelming preoccupation was with perfecting aircraft capable of remaining in the air and improving their performance.

Neither the Wright brothers nor Blériot ever used a parachute, nor did any other pioneer of flight up to the First World War. In the first decade of flight, more than 300 pilots the world over lost their lives. Two in every five of these had fallen more than 300 feet, which was reckoned a sufficient height for the safe operation of the parachute. Thus equipped, they could have survived.

Though their moment had not yet arrived, parachute designers were not idle. In America, Ralph Carhart as early as 1905 laid unofficial claim to using his own free-type parachute. The canopy was stored in a chest pack, and a small pilot parachute lay on top of that. It was a primitive affair, but practicable. The pack was held closed by safety pins which Carhart had to undo when he dropped into space. The pilot 'chute filled out and tugged the larger one from the container.

Charlie Broadwick, a balloon jumper bent on providing greater thrills for his public, made a virtue of a piece of parachute trickery. He made his parachute pack as unobtrusive as he was able, so that the crowd would see him apparently parachute-less. Then suddenly the canopy billowed open, drawn out by a rope 'static line' attached to the balloon by a delicate system of thin thread. He used it hundreds of times and found it far more reliable than established parachutes which occasionally fouled or failed to open.

An adaptation of Broadwick's parachute was to save the life of his daughter Georgia ('Tiny') years later. She was taking part in an aerial display at the World's Fair at San Francisco in 1915 when the wings of the plane she was flying in collapsed. Before the plane crashed, killing the pilot, Tiny leapt out wearing one of her father's parachutes and was saved.

Women have always figured prominently among dare-devil parachutists, and it is worth digressing here to describe an adventure that befell two of them, Daisy Sheppard and Louise May, a novice jumper, in 1908.

The pair were due to perform a twin parachute jump from a balloon near Uttoxeter, Staffordshire, according to a contemporary account published, strangely enough, in the *Pittsburg Leader*. Daisy describes the experience of that day with a vivid realism, offering at the same time an insight into the sensations of ballooning and jumping in those times.

Our start was the same delightful thrill it always is to me. You can't imagine the strange emotion that seizes you for one instant just as the bag makes its first jump. It is the instant when every cry has ceased. The seller of sandwiches chokes in the midst of his shout and there is absolute silence save one sound. It is like the 'A-ah' that a crowd gives when a rocket explodes, only fainter, softer and less self-conscious. . .

We sailed away from the staring faces each on our trapeze about five feet apart. The cheering broke out and lasted until we were so high that we couldn't tell a man from a woman except by a parasol or the colour of her dress.

As the cheering died away, a hollow, stuffy voice close at hand said: 'Isn't it time to drop now?' . . . I looked down again.

We were nearly 4,000 feet from the ground. As this was the height at which we were supposed to descend I turned to Miss May and said: 'Yes, you had better drop first, and if you hurry up I think you can hit that nice smooth lawn the other side of the windmill down there'.

Miss May was a novice . . . and I admired her coolness as she smiled, poised herself carefully on the trapeze. But the smile faded when she pulled the rope and nothing happened. She twitched it again and again, finally pulling with all her might. The trigger spring which should have released a parachute was tangled up with a loose rope from the balloon. . .

I was powerless to do more than advise. We were now nearly 7,000 feet up, and rising rapidly towards a small 'dry' cloud several thousand feet above us. 'You will have to untie your left hand, climb up the side of the balloon and clear that loose rope from the trigger.'

But Louise hadn't enough strength to climb up and detach the trigger.

I told her in as matter-of-fact tone as I could to get her trapeze swaying sideways until it should touch mine, and then she could come down with me in my parachute. She did her best, but somehow it didn't come near enough. . .

The two girls were by now full of fear and doubt—and two miles up. If one of them dropped, the other would go farther up and probably die through lack of oxygen or drift out to sea.

Just then things grew dim and damp as we entered the edge of a cloud. Miss May's nerve was heightened for the moment by having the awful depth below cut out by a cloud, and before I realised, she had done a brave and skilful thing.

Springing from her bar, she leaped the gap to my trapeze and landed on my knees, slipped and saved herself by catching my ankle until I could pull her up. I guided her hands to the ropes, on each side, and pulled my release rope. It worked and down we plunged.

A blast of wind seemed to fly upwards at us and the bar hung

limp beneath. At first I thought the parachute had failed to open
and our death was certain. . .

The rate of descent was slackening now, yet the parachute was
still not fully inflated and the ground was not far below.

A little clump of green under our feet disintegrated as it
grew. Half a dozen foreshortened trees seemed to step away
like those little Japanese flowers which well up the instant they
touch water. . .
   I can remember the concussion, and then there was a blank
until help arrived and they had lifted Miss May from me.

Louise was in fact unhurt, but Daisy did not escape so easily.
Her injury was paralysis of the spine, yet within a few weeks she
announced she would be making parachute descents again.
   'I love it,' she said. 'But I don't think I would care to ride in one
of those new aeroplanes that just skim the ground. We balloonists
look down upon the aeroplane men just as a deep-sea sailor does
upon the crew of a ferryboat.'
   An equally terrifying experience happened to A. E. Gaudron at
Trieste during the first decade of this century. He was scheduled
to make a jump from a parachute attached to the netting of the
balloon by a thin cord which would break when he left the rope
sling. Through a misunderstanding, the parachute was pulled off
the netting and the balloon soared up with Gaudron sitting on the
sling. It quickly dawned on Gaudron that because the balloon had
no valve to let out gas, he had no means of descent. His daring
answer to this, a mile and a half out to sea and 4,000 feet up was
to climb stealthily up the netting and tip the balloon upside down
so that the gas poured out of the neck. Gaudron came down about
three miles out to sea and was picked up by a steamer.
   In 1907, A. Leo Stevens, an American, took the first step towards a fully free-fall parachute. He devised a new type, whose
unique feature was a ripcord, the canopy being jerked out of the
pack by whalebone springs. Not for several years was anyone enterprising enough to try it out from an aircraft; in the

meantime, deaths from air accidents were rising so steeply that in April 1910 a Frenchman, Colonel Lalance, instituted a 5,000-francs prize to be awarded in a competition to the inventor of a parachute which could be dropped with a dead weight of 100 kilograms from a height of 200 metres—about 620 feet—and show the slowest rate of descent.

There was a disappointing lack of response, and it was not until the colonel doubled his prize the following year that inventors began to take notice. One competitor, Monsieur Bonnet of Grasse, demonstrated his parachute at Saint-Cloud on March 16, 1912, from the balloon 'Hélène'. Beneath it was a model of an aeroplane fuselage, about 20 feet long, and there the parachute was stowed, with a dummy in the cockpit. When Bonnet cut the cable over Charmentray, the parachute opened, the fuselage crashed, but the dummy seated inside landed without a mark.

Fifteen days earlier, the first parachute jump was made from an aircraft flying at full speed. At this period, loss of equilibrium was considered to be an aircraft's biggest danger, so Thomas Benoist, the owner of an aviation school in Kinloch Park, St Louis, decided to promote a parachute jump from a flying aeroplane—a feat hitherto thought either impossible or crazy. The guinea-pig was Captain Albert Berry, son of a balloonist and himself a professional parachute jumper.

Twice the attempt had to be delayed because of bad weather. Then on March 1 the aircraft, a Benoist 'pusher' biplane piloted by Antony Jannus and carrying Berry, took off from Kinloch and flew eighteen miles to the army post of Jefferson Barracks on the other side of St Louis, where the attempt was to be made.

The parachute was carried in a galvanised iron cone fixed to the undercarriage, its mouth facing the back of the aircraft until just before the drop. From the mouth emerged two ropes connecting with a trapeze bar, which had two leg loops at its ends.

The plane, travelling at about 55 m.p.h., soared to 1,500 feet. With the drop seconds away, Berry hinged down the metal cone, climbed down through the fuselage frame to the axle and put his legs through the loops. He tied a belt round his waist and then cut himself away, his weight drawing the 'chute out of the container. It was a perfect drop.

'The experience,' said Berry on landing, 'confirms the feasibility of such descents. I dropped fully 500 feet before the parachute opened, and admit to feeling uneasy. But, really, the greatest danger was to the pilot of the plane. I am glad he came out of that successfully.' The reference to the pilot was prompted by a fear that the sudden loss in weight might disturb the aircraft's stability, though Jannus later denied any ill-effects whatever.

For Benoist, pleasure at Berry's success was tempered with some disappointment: first, because he arrived at Jefferson just too late to see the jump; second, had the pair taken up an official barograph with them, they would probably have been able to chalk up two American records—for altitude with a passenger and for rapid climbing without a passenger.

Berry repeated his jump nine days later, this time in public. It was a bitterly cold day, with strong winds and enough snow to mar visibility. So that the spectators could see the performance, Berry dropped from 800 feet, a gesture which nearly cost him his life. The parachute got below him at one point and he was almost wrapped in the canopy. Although he reached ground safely, he vowed he would never jump again—unless the financial rewards were more worthwhile.

In France, Monsieur Bonnet, much encouraged by the success of his experiment at Saint-Cloud, announced a new and more ambitious one at Buc airfield, with a human being and from a plane in flight. The jumper was Adolphe Pégoud, who would both fly and jump solo. When the police heard of this, they tried to ban it, but the mayor intervened and the show went on. Among the spectators was Pégoud's flying teacher, Louis Blériot, whose flight across the Channel back in 1909 had won him the *Daily Mail*'s £1,000 prize.

Pégoud took off in his plane at seven in the evening of August 19, 1913, climbed to 750 feet, set the controls, put the plane into a dive and allowed the deploying parachute to pull him from the cockpit. Within a few seconds he had made a safe if graceless landing in the top of a tree.

The watching Blériot was as fascinated by the plane's behaviour after Pégoud's exit as he was appreciative of his pupil's jump. For the plane sailed on, embarked on a neat loop-the-loop, then made a perfect landing on its own, suffering only trifling damage. At Blériot's suggestion, the loop-the-loop (piloted version) became one of Pégoud's regular stunts. He performed it the following month, having been beaten to the global honour of being the first of all time by a Russian, Nesterov, at Kiev, on the day of the Buc jump.

Pégoud's parachute descent with the Bonnet parachute nevertheless made him the first to do so from an aircraft in Europe, and as a result, Monsieur Bonnet's silk parachute gained considerable prestige, largely on account of its speedy and automatic deployment. It was of the 'soaring' type, the canopy billowing out behind and above the aircraft, the pilot being plucked from his seat by the parachute's drag. Also helping the canopy to open were spring-loaded devices and a pneumatic ring round the canopy's circumference which could be blown up with compressed air whenever the pilot chose.

In 1910 and 1911 Robert Esnault-Pelterie and Gaston Hervieu had tried to adapt parachutes to aircraft. Esnault-Pelterie devised an anti-shock belt which could be connected to a parachute by elastic bands and was fitted with a ripcord release. It was an exceptionally compact device, weighing a mere fifteen pounds and folding into a flat parcel over the back of the fuselage.

Unlike Bonnet's parachute, with its compressed air belt, Hervieu's incorporated metal springs. When packed in a box, the lid closed and compressed the coils; when opened, the skirts unfolded within a second. Its main disadvantage, however, was its complexity.

It received trials at Boulogne in 1910, and tests a year later from the Eiffel Tower before the Ligue Nationale Aérienne with a mock-up aeroplane and dummy figure. The parachute, fixed to

Robert Cocking's portrait (*right*) as it
appeared on a pamphlet sold in aid
of his widow in 1837. In 1911, Franz
Reichelt in his 'parachute overcoat'
(*top*) was killed jumping from the
Eiffel Tower. Three years later
William Newell made the first parachute
descent from an aircraft in Britain.
He jumped from the specially constructed seat on which he is
sitting in the photograph above.

Leslie Irvin (*above left*)
was the first man to jump
with a modern ripcord
parachute, in 1919. Major
Orde-Lees (*above right*),
First World War parachute
pioneer, liked appearing at
demonstrations wearing a
hat to show how easy parachute jumping was (a picture
from his daughter's collection).
In 1917 he jumped successfully from Tower Bridge on
the same occasion as his
colleague (*right*), the Hon.
Lt. A. E. Bowen.

a collapsible trapeze behind the pilot's seat, spread out at the pull of a lever.

It is interesting to see how often inventors during this period relied on artificial aids like compressed air and springs to inflate the canopies. Baldwin and Van Tassell, proponents of the un-ribbed parachute, realised years before that air pressure did the job perfectly well, and proved it.

The failure of a parachute to open was of course a very real fear. It happened, for example, to Madame Cayat de Castella, a woman parachutist, in Brussels in July 1914—a failure that George Prensiel tried to prevent with his compressed air apparatus, faintly resembling an ejection scat.

Not only would it fully open the parachute at the required moment, but it forced it and whatever was attached to it well clear of the aircraft. There were two containers, one containing com-pressed air, the other storing the parachute and attached to the pilot's seat. When the valve of the first cylinder was opened, compressed air filled the parachute container, shooting it out and the pilot's seat with it.

But despite the increasing ingenuity of serious pioneers, the foolhardy still put in their fatal appearances from time to time. Franz Reichelt, an Austrian tailor, followed in the Cocking tradition by seeking to try out a combined parachute and overcoat —his own patent—from the Eiffel Tower. He had assured the authorities that the drop would be only a dummy one, but when he reached the first platform of the Tower, he hooked himself instead of the dummy on to the harness and leapt 180 feet to his death when the parachute failed to open.

Efforts to provide means for saving the plane as well as the pilot continued. Monsieur Mayoux, another French inventor, devised a double parachute, one in each of two tubes. In an emergency, the pilot opened a tap to a compressed air reservoir. The first parachute was thrust out and pulled the pilot with it, then the second, intended for the plane, would open. However, Eiffel Tower tests saved a dummy pilot but crashed a model plane.

Captain M. Couade, a French engineer, went even further wi

a single portmanteau device intended to save pilot and plane *together.* The silken parachute was to be placed inside a tube projecting from the rear of the plane. A small pilot 'chute was launched into the wind, hauling out the main one, the heaviest part of which was under the pilot. This ambitious idea was probably saved from costly failure by the intervention of the Great War.

Throughout the nineteenth century, France had maintained a strong lead in ballooning and parachuting while, in Britain, Sir George Cayley worked on the development of the aeroplane. Now France was to be overtaken in her progress with the parachute by the U.S.A., and later by Germany.

The most promising man-carrying parachute at this time appeared to be Leo Stevens' 'Life Pack' which, in its 1912 form, with an independent instead of a rope-attached ripcord (for forgetful jumpers!), received a thorough testing at the hands of Rodman Law, a steeplejack who had jumped with similar-style products from the Statue of Liberty, bridges and other high buildings.

Stevens' parachute pack, weighing only 25 pounds, was held closed by piano wire strung through the tips of metal cones inserted through eyelets in the flaps—a remarkably similar system to that used today. A sturdy tug on the ring attached to a cord looped over the jumper's shoulder rapidly slid out the piano wire, and the flaps, with springy whalebone embedded, flew open and the canopy was pulled out.

Harry B. Brown, who flew a Wright biplane from which Rodman Law jumped in October 1912, commented: 'In my mind, not as an exhibition stunt, but as a safety factor, it is the greatest move which has yet been made towards the aviator's safety. You can readily see if a machine were to get on fire or break in two how secure the aviator and his passenger would be; [and] by merely rolling off or falling off, descend with perfect safety.'

But Stevens' design was apparently too far ahead of its time; so was Charlie Broadwick's 'Patent Safety Pack Vest', a knapsack-type pack with harness straps stitched to a close-fitting canvas jacket and worn on the back. Latterly, too, it was operated by a ripcord. Testing the newer version one day, Broadwick came down on it so easily that he took out a packet of cigarettes and casually puffed his way to earth.

Daughter 'Tiny' was similarly blasé. In 1913 she had become the first woman to parachute from an aircraft; one year later, she gave a dazzling display before visiting Congressmen and senior officers of the U.S. Army. As a result they ordered a few of Broadwick's products for testing, but no more. As far as they were concerned, parachutes were still simply 'props' for circus acts, without serious purpose.

Hand in hand with the increase in the popularity of flying, deaths from air accidents jumped alarmingly: 29 in 1910, 79 in 1911, 104 in 1912. The figures disturbed aeronautic experts and fliers alike and the case for parachutes was repeatedly argued. But the stock reply was always handy—that in very few cases would a parachute have helped. Most fatal accidents, it was claimed, occurred too near the ground—during the landing process—for a parachute to have time to operate.

Preoccupation was with causes: inexperience of the pilot, reckless flying, faulty construction of the machine (a favourite target for blame). So there were calls for tightening up on construction standards, ensuring the plane's equilibrium, and improvement of the judgment and skill of pilots through proper training. But still there was no provision for escape in emergencies.

Thus it was possible in 1914 for members of that learned and distinguished body the Royal Aeronautical Society to hear a lecture on 'Lessons Accidents Have Taught' by a Fellow, Colonel H. C. L. Holden, in which due emphasis was given to the safety belt, helmet, the need for medical examination, good aircraft design and sound repair-work, but without a single reference to the possibility of escape by parachute, either during discourse or discussion.

With the approach of war, parachutes, their few far-sighted advocates, and their designers ceased to make news, both in

Britain and America. After all, in war-time aircraft were used for fighting, not as jumping-off points for parachutists.

The refusal to recognise the parachute's potentialities was almost unbelievable. The Royal Flying Corps had been founded in April 1912, and in September 1913, less than a year before the Great War erupted in Europe, *Flight* magazine declared its position: 'Frankly, we see very little future for the parachute as a life-saving apparatus in emergency on aeroplanes; with dirigibles it might be another matter. . .

'Nevertheless, we are far from dissuading the ingenious inventor from persevering with his attempts to devise a really satisfactory folding parachute that can be applied to the body in a moment, and that will open out with absolute certainty when the person jumps into the air.

'. . . We fancy that there may be more to be said for the ability to intentionally leave an aeroplane that is in perfect control than for the possible virtue of the parachute as a means of checking an aviator's fall in the event of disaster.'

Not much encouragement there for the aspirant. Yet there were people around with faith to feed the enterprising, and people around to try to meet the need. One was a retired railway engineer named Everard Calthrop, the inventor of the British 'Guardian Angel' parachute, who found a cause and lost a fortune (see Chapter Six).

One of its early champions was 'Professor' William Newell, who on May 9, 1914, used it to become the first Englishman to jump from an aircraft in flight. Newell was an experienced aeronaut and parachutist, and it seems he had few qualms about the oddly casual way the feat was to be performed. It took place one evening at Hendon airfield from a five-seater 100 horse-power Graham-White aerobus biplane. With the moral support of another parachutist, Frank Goodden, Newell set about trying to find a suitable jumping off point on the plane. Because a passenger seat was not practicable, he had eventually to settle for the port chassis skid.

A crude rope seat was improvised between the front and

diagonal skid struts, and there sat Newell, determined and dignified, with the 'Guardian Angel', carefully folded and tied with a breaking cord, on his lap.

At 7.45 p.m. the aerobus took off, with Reginald Carr as pilot and Goodden and R. J. Lillywhite as passengers. It climbed for 18 minutes to a height of 2,000 feet, and then Newell, assisted by a friendly kick from Goodden, jumped off. Almost immediately, the parachute filled out and, after some swinging, steadied and brought Newell down in under $2\frac{1}{2}$ minutes with three cheers from a small crowd ringing in his ears.

Newell said afterwards that he did not remember Goodden's 'kick'; that in fact he was so cold that he could not tell whether he was standing on the skid or not!

In recognition of this exploit, the London Aeronautical Club awarded him a silver medal. But Newell's praises were not sung by the public at large, and in the national newspapers the event received only a few paragraphs.

6

ORDEAL BY FIRE

W AS N EWELL's drop to be the signal for the general adoption of the parachute for pilots? It was not. Indifference to its value as an escape device was to persist and infect the entire 1914–18 air war on the Allies' side. To our shame, it was the Germans, in the last year of war, who were to exploit the parachute, saving scores of their pilots' lives as a result.

Parachutes were used by the Allies, but only by front-line kite balloon observers, who were highly vulnerable to air attack. The parachute was the attached type, fixed to the balloon basket and hauled from its bag by the jumper's weight.

Not all Allied pilots wanted them, of course. Many regarded them with contempt, as if carrying a parachute were an admission of weakness. But even the many who looked upon parachutes as a sensible precaution were prevented by the air authorities from using them.

The reasons were two-fold: first, it was widely, and cynically, thought that pilots with parachutes might abandon their planes too easily. To echo a comment in *Flight* magazine in 1913: 'A pilot's job is to stick to his aeroplane'—even, it seems, unto death. Secondly, because parachutes fell some way short of perfection in design and adaptability, they were considered unsuitable for aircraft use. Thus half a chance of survival took second place to no chance at all.

Parachutes had of course existed in America for some years. Yet Broadwick's 'Patent Safety Pack Vest', and Leo Stevens' trusty 'Life Pack' had vanished into obscurity in the United States, and their pilots were not allowed to use parachutes either. But the Broadwick and the Stevens had been widely publicised over there through performance and in the pages of specialist journals, which makes unawareness on both sides of the Atlantic all the more extraordinary. Lack of interest in Stevens eventually drove him to make attached-type parachutes for balloonists.

With interest and encouragement from those in positions of power, parachutes could undoubtedly have been provided for all who needed them. Instead, there was a contemptible lack of faith in expertise or in pilots' loyalty or intelligence—pilots typified by Sholto Douglas, who went on to become Marshal of the RAF, Lord Douglas of Kirtleside.

Lord Douglas did not discover the tacit ban on parachutes until shortly before the publication of his autobiography, *Years of Combat*,[1] in 1963. The anguish was still there after half a century.

> When I . . . thought about what we had had to endure and I recalled how so many men had died in such agony—all because somebody had thought so little of us that they believed that providing us with parachutes would encourage us to abandon our aircraft—my anger was roused in a way that is unusual for me.

The fear that was constantly with the front-line pilot was that of fire in the air, Lord Douglas recalls. One of the most unpleasant of any airman's experiences was to have to witness the helplessness of a friend going down in flames.

> On one patrol early in 1917 I was flying in formation with my squadron when we were suddenly attacked by some Huns. After the first flurry was over I glanced across at the next aircraft beside me in our formation, and I saw that the observer, poor devil, was standing up in the back seat agitatedly trying to call the attention of his pilot to a glint of flame that was just starting to appear along the side of their aircraft. A moment later there was a violent explosion and the whole aircraft disintegrated. Such a sight was all too common in our flying of those days, and so far as I was concerned it was one of the most horrible that one could witness.

To observers in balloons, sent up to track enemy movements or

[1] Published by Collins.

direct artillery fire at the front, parachutes were salvation indeed. During the war, 800 of them, including seventy-six Americans, came to owe their lives to the flimsy sheet of silk, the British version of which was the attached-type Spencer, packed in a characteristic 'candle extinguisher' container slung on the side of the basket.

Even then there were scores of casualties, among them the famous music hall comedian Basil ('Gilbert the Filbert') Hallam, who made a fatal error during an enemy aircraft attack. Hallam jumped to his death believing that he was still tied to his parachute, which had actually detached itself.

Balloons were all too easy targets. German fighters swept in and strafed them with tracer and sent them blazing to earth. Retaliation with rifle fire, at first a routine gesture, was soon abandoned because it delayed escape, often crucially. And if the jumper failed to get clear quickly enough, the balloon's flaming bag was likely to drop straight on to him.

Officers training for balloon work could volunteer for a practice drop from a captive balloon if they wished, and many did so. One balloon officer, Stephen Wilkinson, wrote after the war: 'It required no small amount of nerve to make the effort, and when the actual moment arrived and the jumper looked down to earth about 2,000 feet below there were many cases of wind-up, and we used to put the final touch on by a sudden shove off the side of the basket. The effect of a jump on the remaining occupant left in the basket was rather alarming.'[1]

Sitting targets as they were, these balloonists often displayed immense coolness and gallantry. In August 1916 a balloon observer, 2nd Lieut. A. G. D. Gavin, was awarded the D.S.O. for 'conspicuous presence of mind and unselfish courage' in the use of a parachute. When his balloon broke loose and headed quickly for the enemy lines, Gavin explained to his passenger how to use the parachute and helped him out of the basket. Then he destroyed all his papers and came down on his own parachute, landing in a hail of enemy gunfire. Both survived.

[1] *Lighter Than Air* (A. H. Stockwell, 1930).

But for the parachute, casualties among balloon observers would have been enormous. Something of the grimness of the ordeal is captured in this German account.

[The balloon observer] must never allow himself to be disturbed by the thought that, if his balloon were set on fire above him, he would have a few seconds only in which to make his leap for safety with his parachute. As he was unable to see and form any judgment, he had to rely on the officer on ground duty to give him the order to jump. When this order came through the telephone, he had to jump from his basket into the depths below without a second's hesitation.

Even then his troubles were not over. The attacking aeroplane would direct a furious fire against the defenceless man hanging from the parachute and blazing tracer bullets would leap at him. Only extraordinary will-power, self-control, strong nerves, and a stout heart enabled him to stand the strain; and to go up again after his descent! Many an infantry officer who had applied for training as a balloon observer in order to have a rest from the hardships of the trenches has said, after an experience of this kind, 'I would sooner undergo a five days' bombardment than make another ascent.'[1]

Much was now to be heard of a parachute named the 'Guardian Angel', invented by the forceful but often tactless Everard Calthrop, who was to be a thorn in the side of Whitehall for years to come.

Calthrop was pursuing a creditable career in engineering before he began working on parachutes. He was apprenticed with the railways in England and in 1882 went out to India. Then in 1910 came a tragedy which switched the course of Calthrop's life. His great motoring friend, the Hon. Charles Rolls (of Rolls-Royce) was flying a Wright biplane in a competition at Bournemouth when the rudder gear snapped and he crashed. To Rolls went the unhappy distinction of being the first Englishman to die in an aircraft accident.

[1] *The German Air Force in the Great War*, G. P. Neumann (Hodder, 1920).

Although Rolls was too low for a parachute to have saved him, the incident, coupled with the narrow flying escapes of Calthrop's own eldest son, impressed on him the need for a good life-saver. He decided to devote the rest of his life to improving parachutes.

After several years' research, the 'Guardian Angel' was created. It was given its first official trial by the Admiralty Air Department at Farnborough two months after war broke out, and was warmly praised for its 'automatic' opening system. But its weight of 90 pounds was a big obstacle.

Drastic modifications resulted in the 'A' type, weighing only 24 pounds, and its length of drop before opening was a mere 80–100 feet. Calthrop's parachute had one overwhelming advantage on other types: 'positive opening': a disc, or in later models a wooden ring, about two feet in diameter, braced the mouth of the parachute so that when hauled from its cone-shaped container by the weight of the falling pilot, air would pour in and deploy it immediately, and without shock. It was the maker's proud claim that the 'Guardian Angel', properly used, never failed to open.

Among the 'Angel's' drawbacks was a vulnerability to enemy fire, because it was stored either under the cockpit or behind the undercarriage. Also, so complex was its meticulously procedured packing that the task took a skilled man up to two hours.

Tests with the 'Guardian Angel' in March 1915 were sufficiently encouraging for Lieut.-Col. Sir Bryan Leighton to drop with it 'live' at low levels. It still failed to be approved for general issue to airmen, but this did not discourage Calthrop. Convinced that orders would soon flood in, he set up a factory in the Edgware Road, London, and formed a private company. Using the combined resources of himself and friends, he had by this time spent an unprofitable £12,000 on research and development. In December 1916, R.F.C. headquarters in France were told the 'Guardian Angel' had been tested by the Admiralty from BE2c planes, and in every case the parachute opened when it had fallen about 100 feet. Its superiority and reliability over other types were acknowledged because not only did it open with minimal shock, but air pressure would build up inside directly the parachute was released, giving it a greater tendency to open; in addition to this, the inventor claimed to have overcome an inclination for the parachute to spin (caused by the ropes unwinding and rewinding as the airman descended). 'No airman,' it was stated, 'has yet made a descent from an aeroplane in one of the parachutes, but several descents have been made from balloons and airships. The inventor claims that they would be most useful for secret service work, and descents at night in the event of a forced landing, as the airman alights so gently.'

The following month, trials were carried out at Orfordness Experimental Station, Suffolk, with the object of dropping secret agents, and some weeks later up to thirty of them, with black canopies and rigging lines to avoid being picked out by searchlights, were dropped behind the German lines in France.

Later they were used for the same purpose on the Italo-Austrian front. In his book, entitled *In the Sideshows*,[1] Captain Wedgwood Benn has described one of these missions, in which he served as navigator and organiser. The intention was to parachute an Italian agent well behind the Austrians. He would then work his way to his native town, gathering information as he went to send back by signal or by one of the carrier pigeons accompanying him.

The plane, an old SP4, carried Lieut.-Col. W. G. Barker V.C. as pilot, Captain Benn as navigator and an Italian named Alessandro Tandura. Fitted with his parachute, Tandura squatted over a trapdoor through which he would disappear on his mission.

The aircraft carried three bombs, two to be dropped on the return journey to disguise the expedition's true purpose, and a third to mislead the enemy in the event of capture.

The mission was an outstanding success. Tandura disappeared, clad in military uniform, and when he reached ground he changed into peasant clothing and for three months sent valuable information back to Italian Command. Eventually he earned the Gold Medal for Valour—the Italian Army's highest award.

The value of parachutes for dropping supplies was not fully

[1] Hodder, 1919.

appreciated until after the war. They were completely overlooked in Mesopotamia in 1916, when attempts were made to relieve General Townshend's troops besieged in Kūt-el-Mara. The call was for at least 5,000 pounds of supplies every day to feed the 12,000 starving soldiers. The method of conveying them was the crude one of dropping canisters from low-flying aircraft to fall bodily onto the ground. For two weeks until the force surrendered, nine aircraft, escorted by five others, shuttled seven tons of food, along with letters, wireless batteries and medical supplies, though much was wasted because many containers burst open on impact.

But such exercises brought no nearer the prospect of saving the lives of airmen in action. Among members of the Air Board, which had dragged its feet ever since the idea of parachutes was first mooted, there was little enthusiasm and some hostility.

Even supposedly informed opinion displayed an alarming naïvety. Totally ignoring the very real dangers of fire, particularly in fighting machines, Borlase Matthews wrote in the 1916 edition of the *Aviation Pocket Book*: '. . . The many suggestions as to the uses of parachutes in aeroplanes do not take account of the fact that in the case of an engine stoppage or the like, the aeroplane itself acts as efficiently as a parachute and has the additional advantage of allowing the landing ground to be chosen.' In the 1917 edition, parachutes were ignored altogether.

In August of that year an unconfirmed report filtered through that a German airman had dropped by parachute and survived. This was seen cautiously by one journal as 'a case for inquiry and within limits experiment, but we should scarcely like to go as far as to say that instructions in the use of the parachute should as yet form a part of the ordinary course of training of aviators'.

And this was 1917, a year of disaster for young pilots under training. According to a subsequent report to Parliament there were no fewer than 800 fatal accidents among flying trainees in 1917, and the public were expected to believe Major John Baird, Parliamentary member of the Air Board, when he told the Commons in March 1918: 'No case is known of any officer under instruction providing or wishing to provide himself with a parachute. Experiments are proceeding, but no parachute suitable for use from an aeroplane has yet been arrived at.'

A strange reply indeed, in the light of Everard Calthrop's subsequent disclosure that over a period of two years many officers had applied direct to his company to buy parachutes, and that 'we informed the Air Board of this and applied for permission to supply them; but sanction was refused'.

Captain R. M. Groves, in a minute to the Air Board, reported: 'The heavier-than-air people all say that they flatly decline to regard the parachute in an aeroplane as a life-saving device worth carrying in its present form.' Just which 'heavier-than-air people' were consulted is not clear: senior officers desk-bound in London, or the pilots who every day were blazing down like meteors over the lines in France?

But there were admirable exceptions to brass-hat distrust of the parachute: for example, Major T. Orde-Lees, future Secretary of the Air Board's Parachute Committee. Orde-Lees was a restless eccentric passionately dedicated to the parachute campaign who attracted considerable unpopularity among his colleagues.

Not that unpopularity bothered him, or that it was a novel experience. He was disliked for his exhibitionism at school, unpopular as a young Royal Marine officer, and when, in 1914, he went out with Shackleton's Imperial Trans-Antarctic Expedition, his facility to alienate himself dogged him there too. At one stage, the ship Endurance broke up and had to be abandoned, and Shackleton left twenty-two members of the expedition on an island to await his return with assistance. But it was three months before he did so, by which time the stranded explorers were in danger of resorting to cannibalism. The question to be decided was: who would be the first to be sacrificed? In the opinion of Frank Wild, leader of the stranded group, one name shone above all the rest. The first choice, unbeknown to him until much later, was Orde-Lees.

Fortunately for Orde-Lees, rescue arrived in time, and he survived to carry out his work on parachutes with great diligence. On Sunday, November 11, 1917, he and the Hon. Lieut. A. E.

Bowen, late of the R.F.C., gave demonstration jumps with the 'Guardian Angel' from Tower Bridge into the Thames 150 feet below, watched by the inventor, Calthrop.

The purpose was first to prove, publicly and beyond doubt, the claim that the parachute could open as low as 200 feet; secondly, to show that Calthrop's quick release device for detaching the harness would work as well in water as it did on land.

Continual delays before the start made Orde-Lees impatient enough to threaten withdrawal. He let himself be persuaded to continue, but only on condition that he could make a head-first dive; feet-first drops reminded him of steep aircraft descents, which he disliked. The 'Guardian Angel', neatly packed in its muffin-shaped bag, hung from a beam sticking six feet out from the upper parapet of the bridge. Orde-Lees wrapped the attaching rope round his right leg and, at a flag-wave from Calthrop, dived down, jerking and somersaulting until the parachute opened. Bowen followed, but feet first in the traditional way. Both jumpers vanished beneath the water, surfaced immediately, thanks to their life-belts, and as the current and breeze carried them downstream, they operated their quick release devices, detached their parachutes and were picked up by a Thames waterman.

In this manner was performed the lowest ever human parachute drop, several hundred feet lower than the previous one—an answer, it might be thought, to those parachute critics who doubted its effectiveness near the ground. It also caught the eye of a public which may not even have been aware of its existence.

The war dragged on. . . In April 1918, the R.F.C. became the RAF. Two months later, Mr Philip Morrell, Liberal M.P. for Burnley, tried as he had done before, to persuade the Air Ministry to supply trainee pilots with parachutes 'if necessary at their own expense and allow them to undergo a course of parachuting during their flying course'

Major Baird stonewalled again. He refused to accept Mr Morrell's fatality figure of 800, taking refuge in a 'much smaller' —but unspecified—total. As for Mr Morrell's suggestions, 'Experiments have been and are still being made, but the great majority of accidents occurred under circumstances which precluded the hope that a parachute would be of any value.'

Because of what Calthrop called impatiently 'the general indifference and passive resistance of the authorities', it was not until June 1918 that the Air Board set up a Parachute Committee. General Maitland, who had jumped from the airship Delta, was appointed chairman, and Major Orde-Lees became secretary.

The following month, Orde-Lees went to France to report on the Spencer-type parachutes used by the kite balloon observers. The Spencers were different from the 'Guardian Angel': attached-type, but not 'positive opening'. A number of accidents occurred while using them, about one in 200 failing to open.

The Spencer harness was unpopular and rarely used because it was not adjustable and became hot and uncomfortable in summer. So each man made his own substitute harness, crude affairs of rope, which they cut with a knife to free themselves on landing. Some roughly made harnesses even had parts held together with trouser buttons. The observers had never heard of the 'Guardian Angel', on the face of it a safer design; and nothing would make them try it out. 'They were sceptical of the devil they don't know and prefer the devil they do,' reported Orde-Lees.

It had been found through experiment that installing a parachute on an aircraft might reduce the plane's speed by two or three miles an hour. Orde-Lees added: 'There is no doubt that the majority of aeroplane pilots desire parachutes irrespective of prejudice to the performance of the machine.'

This contradiction of assertions in the Commons and elsewhere as to whether pilots did or did not want parachutes was further underlined by a comment of Brig.-Gen. Charles Longcroft, who remarked in France that 'as far as he and his pilots were concerned, he strongly desired that some steps should be taken to obtain and test parachutes suitable for aeroplanes. [He] said he had heard the objection that pilots might jump prematurely, but as a practical parachutist himself he did not believe it.'

Orde-Lees told Longcroft later: 'It is very encouraging to find that a senior officer who is both a pilot and parachutist has given this matter so much consideration.' Later, Longcroft took command of the RAF division for training pilots, which suffered enormous casualties in air accidents.

A further impetus to the parachute's advancement was brought about by the death in an air crash in France of one of Britain's leading aces, the newly promoted Squadron Commander, Major James McCudden V.C., whose 'bag' was fifty-seven German aircraft destroyed or shot down out of control, on July 9, 1918. McCudden, a firm supporter of parachute provision on all aircraft, whether home-based or in France, was flying an S.E. 5a to take over his new command, and landed at Auxi-le-Chateau to ask No. 8 Squadron headquarters the way. He climbed back into his plane, and took off. At 700 feet his engine choked and he turned as if to land again. Suddenly he dived into the trees behind the hangars, crashed and was mortally wounded.

'What went wrong may never be known,' one witness said, 'but one wonders whether if he knew his machine was out of control, he might have been saved by a parachute.' And *The Aeroplane* magazine observed: 'One believes firmly that the parachute is as necessary a fitting to an aeroplane as a lifebuoy to a ship, and that it has just as good, or just as slight, a chance of saving lives, according to circumstances. It is not an infallible life preserver, but it is an excellent insurance policy. That fact should make it worthwhile'.

There was no parachute to save the life of the daring and much decorated American ace, Major Raoul Lufbery. On May 19, 1918, he attacked a German triplane over Toul, in France, in his Nieuport at 2,500 feet, then withdrew when his machine-gun jammed. Sweeping in to renew the attack, the Nieuport suddenly burst into flames, and Lufbery was seen to jump out of it and hit the ground a quarter of a mile from where his plane crashed.

The Allies were not yet aware of it, but on the Western Front parachutes were being freely used by German pilots. In June 1918, a little more than a month after Lufbery's death, one saved the life of Ernst Udet, the famous German fighter pilot with 62 confirmed victories to his credit. Udet was flying his Fokker over Villers when he took on a Breguet carrying out artillery observation. As the crippled French plane went into a dive, Udet chased it down, only to receive a burst at point-blank range from the doomed French gunner.

His own petrol tank now smashed, Udet dropped over the side on his parachute and landed in no-man's-land with a twisted ankle. He crawled 200 yards to the safety of the German lines.

The establishment of a British Parachute Committee so late in the war, coupled with attempts to fit the parachutes on aircraft simply not built for them, seemed doomed to futility.

Calthrop's parachute was certainly an ingenious piece of craftsmanship, and way ahead of anything so far produced in Britain. It was so packed that nothing was left to chance. When pulled out by the weight of the pilot, first came the rigging tapes, carefully folded so that punching or entanglement was impossible. The canopy, which followed it, was so pleated and folded that the longest time taken to open after the jump was two and a half seconds. There was even a shock absorber to cushion the strain on the jumper's body when the 'chute opened.

It gave an impressive enough performance for a firm of Lloyds underwriters to offer to cut insurance premiums for pilots by twenty per cent, provided they confined their flying to planes equipped with the 'Guardian Angel'; moreover *Flight* magazine revised the unfavourable opinion expressed four years earlier, and commented:

> The fact that a perusal of the, unfortunately, only too frequent accidents to aviators would indicate that a very great percentage of these pilots might have been saved had they been equipped with a reliable parachute is a very strong point in favour of a more general adoption of this useful accessory. We do not doubt that there are a good many people who shrug their shoulders at the idea of a parachute on board an aeroplane. We were inclined to do the same—until we saw Mr Calthrop's 'Guardian Angel.'

The dangers of air accidents were eloquently stated when the plane flown by Major Bannatyne D.S.O., caught fire at 1,000 feet after engine failure near Cirencester. To escape the flames creeping along the fuselage, he climbed out of the cockpit and crawled along to the tail, from which he hung by his hands till the flames reached him again. Just before the machine crashed, he dropped clear, surviving with only a broken arm and cuts.

Fire was a perennial hazard on both sides. Without a parachute, all the air-crew could do was to come to terms with the risk and cope as best they could. Second-Lieut. Leslie Pargeter, who was transferred from the infantry to the R.F.C. late in the war and flew as an observer in two-seater R.E.8 biplanes with Army Co-operation, told the author of two missions in the summer of 1918 during which the petrol tank was badly damaged.

On an observation sortie with the army, the R.E.8 dropped several bombs on the German lines, then returned to its scheduled task. 'There was a lot of Archie [anti-aircraft fire] about,' recalled Pargeter (who is now, at the time of writing, eighty years of age), 'and suddenly, when we were at about 6,000 feet there came a loud crack. The petrol tank had been hit by a shell fragment and there was petrol everywhere. The pilot and I were drenched in it. Immediately, of course, one thought of the possibility of fire. So I hopped out on to the lower wing and stuffed my glove into the hole in the tank, which is forward of the pilot. Then we set off for home and managed to land without further trouble.'

A similar incident occurred three weeks later, when they spotted a group of Germans on the ground and swung into the attack, the pilot firing his Vickers as the R.E.8 dived, Pargeter with the swivelling Lewis from the rear as the plane zoomed. The Germans promptly retaliated. 'Soon the petrol tank had caught it again—we were as full of machine-gun bullet holes as an old watering can,' said Pargeter. 'I dropped over the side onto the wing once again and plugged the holes with as many fingers as I could. Fortunately, we managed to touch down before running out of petrol.'

This time Pargeter and his pilot earned a general's congratulations for helping to restore contact between infantry units that had lost touch with each other, Pargeter receiving the D.F.C. for his exploits. The citation, which he modestly refrained from mentioning, described him as 'a very gallant officer'.

'In these planes,' said Pargeter, 'fire was our third passenger. If we'd caught fire and had parachutes, we'd have used them. But of course we never had them.'

In fact, his only experience of parachutes was in carrying out experiments for dropping supplies to forward troops. Pargeter remembers trying, though admittedly with little success, to drop boxes of parachute-borne ammunition in August 1918, from underneath the engine nacelle of an R.E.8.

'We didn't know the first thing about parachutes,' he said. 'In one case, when I pulled the release lever, the parachute didn't open and the box just shot down through the roof of a hangar, damaging the wings of two aircraft. Then we circled around the base and dropped the other, and the parachute opened beautifully. The trouble was, after I had released it I noticed the padre below, having a nice afternoon bath behind his hut. For a horrible moment I thought it was going to hit him. It missed, but fell onto the roof behind him, and his hut immediately collapsed!'

★

In the middle of August 1918 the Air Ministry received a severe jolt, when the rumoured use of parachutes by the Germans was confirmed. Three definite cases were reported of escapes with the aid of white silk parachutes by German pilots from burning Fokkers over the Western front. A few weeks later an American air force pursuit group shot down eleven German planes, and all the pilots landed safely by parachute.

When the Allies captured one, they found it was stuffed into a 10-inch-thick sack on which the pilot sat. It was designed by Otto Heinecke and a static line was used to deploy the canopy, to which was attached a breaker-cord which snapped with the pilot's weight as he dropped. Later, Heinecke developed an improvement on the 'Guardian Angel', with a back-pack type 'chute hauled out by a cord attached to the plane. The first parachutes were of Japanese silk, but later captures revealed cruder forms of calico. These parachutes may not have been ideal, but they saved lives: that was what mattered.

Germany had won no mean moral victory over the Allies with her aeroplane parachute, and many of our fliers wondered why they too were not similarly equipped. So the tardy, tortuous process of testing was visibly speeded up: in England the 'Guardian Angel' and Mears; in America the silk and cotton versions of their A.E.F.; in France the Robert, packed into a clumsy bundle with a lanyard projecting from the centre like an apple stalk, the whole thing being strapped to a three-ply board on the pilot's back. All were of the static line type.

Parachute campaigners were filled with fresh enthusiasm. Brig.-Gen. Robert Brooke-Popham, in charge of supplies in France, demanded news of progress in London. He sought suggestions from unit commanders in the field as to how parachutes could be fixed to fighters. The ideas multiplied: under the wings, on the side of the fuselage, in an enlarged locker behind the pilot's seat, on the fuselage behind the pilot's shoulders. 'It would be easier to give more definite suggestions', wrote the commander of one aeroplane supply depot sardonically, 'if I actually had a parachute.'

The Germans had simply provided themselves with a parachute, taken a chance and jumped. The wings of Allied progress seemed overloaded with problems in the search for elusive perfection. Much thought and effort went into ways of fitting them on to aircraft. At Farnborough they succeeded with the S.E.5, Sopwith Snipe, Bristol Fighter and D.H.9; the 'Camel', however, proved difficult because there was no space in the cockpit, and the fuselage behind the petrol tanks was unsafe due to the fire-risk. On September 23, a group including Winston Churchill, then Minister of Munitions, watched parachute trials with the Bristol Fighter. In one case the parachute caught on the tail-skid.

The process of fitting and testing with dummy drops on individual types of aircraft, with delays, reports, second thoughts, re-testing and report back, would clearly take months. Nevertheless, in September, an order for 500 'Guardian Angels', duly modified, had by then been placed with Calthrop. All single-seater fighters, ordered Brooke-Popham, would be fitted with parachutes in France.

Test drops were now made comparing the 'Guardian Angel' with the Mears, a cheaper parachute which was rolled up in a pack on the pilot's back, a cord being attached from it to the plane's body. The simple pack was intended to cope with the problem of dropping out of the plane at speed; also, it could be rolled into various widths to suit the dimensions of varying sized cockpits. Although it was not 'positive opening', it was considered good enough for 500 to be ordered.

With the help of an RAF officer and a young engineer, Calthrop set about improving release equipment. A pilot parachute and a main parachute were separately housed in compartments in the fuselage and so arranged that the compartment containing the pilot chute could be opened to the airstream. The canopy blossomed and hauled out the main parachute.

In October 1918 Sir William Bull, Conservative M.P. for Hammersmith, finally drew a public admission from the Government that parachutes were effective as an aircraft safety device. In the House of Commons he asked the Under-Secretary of State to the Air Ministry 'whether any report has been received as to the use of parachutes by German airmen as a means of escape from injured aeroplanes; and whether the tenor of the report, if any, indicates that the appliance is effective in life-saving'. Major Baird: 'The reply to both parts of the question is in the affirmative.'

Two days later the German aeronautical journal *Flug Sport*, noting the immense prejudice against parachutes in Britain, published a detailed illustrated article on the 'Guardian Angel'.

The parachute section of the Air Force Technical Department was now receiving sufficient misguided ideas for parachutes to have to publish a notice giving guidance to inventors. This emphasised that, given the fulfilment of basic requirements of size (28 feet flat diameter), weight (under 40 pounds, including harness) and rapid production, choice would be governed mainly by considerations of morale.

Parachutes depending on an explosive charge, springs, or compressed air for their liberation and deployment were ruled out because they could too easily fail. 'This preys on an aviator's mind, and although "half a parachute" is better than no parachute he will only feel justified in taking greater flying liberties when he knows that the action of his parachute is independent of the functioning of such devices. In short, the simpler the parachute the better.'

Inventors were admonished for ignoring the psychological side of parachutes, which had above all to provide the pilot with confidence. Yet inventors 'seem to regard aviators much in the same way as we regard animals used for experimental purposes—as being without cognizance of the dangers to which they are to be subjected'.

All this discussion, though prompted by the noblest motives, came a trifle late for the war pilots. By now, thousands of their burned and broken bodies were lying buried under the skies from which they had plunged—men for whom half a parachute would certainly have been an improvement, in the technical department's phrase, on no parachute at all. So Armistice Day on November 11 came and went, the cheering and the shouting died, and aircraft as well as swords began to be beaten into ploughshares; the 'Guardian Angel' and the Mears gathered cobwebs, and Major Orde-Lees would arrive home to weep at his Whitehall colleagues' blind intransigence.

Experimentation continued but, shamefully, so did the opposition. Yet almost daily the need for parachutes was stressed by reports of deaths on training flights. In January 1919, Orde-Lees saw a young officer, Lieut. Christopher Berkeley, killed while giving instruction at Northolt, Middlesex. He was the only regular pilot who had ever made a parachute jump from an aircraft. 'It is therefore especially tragic', wrote Orde-Lees, 'that he should have met his death in an accident where a parachute might reasonably have been expected to save his life.' And he added: 'It being the opinion of a good many senior officers and squadron commanders that parachutes are not likely to be of any useful service on training machines, the account of Lieut. Berkeley's death is appended. . .'

As the work of adaptation ground tediously on, Calthrop counted his losses: £20,000 and an unreckonable sum in terms of patience and exasperation. Released from the obligatory wartime vow of silence, Calthrop issued in March 1919 an advertising brochure which was also a declaration of faith and an exposé of official inertia. Never one for diplomatic finesse, Calthrop laid into the Service Establishment with gusto and obvious disgust, with the exception of officers like the handful of Maitlands and Orde-Leeses who had consistently championed him in particular or the parachute in general.

'The work now being done by the Parachute Committee and other departments of the British Air Ministry', Calthrop pointed out, 'is precisely that which we continually begged the air authorities to undertake from as far back as July 1916.'

On the specific official view that deaths in the air during training were inevitable, Calthrop said: '. . . It has apparently struck no-one . . . of those professing to take a special interest in the Air Force, to inquire into these casualties to ascertain whether the means did not exist by which they might be reduced'.

Calthrop quotes a senior officer as saying, during the war, 'We can't force a thing like this on our youngsters. If they want it, they will ask for it.'

The only answer to that now lies with the ghosts of 6,000 British air force dead.

7

BIRTH OF FREE-FALL

HOW MANY British pilots were sacrificed to the consequences of official inaction over parachutes in the First World War it is impossible to say. But at least 250 are known to have hurled themselves from their burning aircraft in final desperate attempts to choose the quicker death; countless others crashed with their planes who might have survived had the parachute not been the mistrusted and underdeveloped novelty it was.

Now, catching the heady mood of victory, the showmen took the stage again. William Newell, the first Englishman to jump from a moving aircraft in 1914, repeated his demonstration at Hendon on Whit Monday, 1919, this time with two parachutes in case one was not impressive enough. In September he appeared in the role of hot-air balloon stuntman at a Victory Sports display at Harrow, coupling a hair-raising act with a further double parachute drop.

Newell's act was worthy of the nineteenth-century showmen. He dug a long trench and covered it with iron sheeting and a layer of earth. At one end he lit a wood fire, from which the heat and smoke passed through into a balloon at the other. When the balloon filled out with hot air, he perched on the sling of the attached parachute and was swept high into the air until he cut himself loose, opening one parachute and picturesquely descending on the second.

Women jumpers, like the attractive 19-year-old Sylva Boyden, 'the English Air Girl', were still often in the public eye. Sylva was introduced to parachuting by Major Orde-Lees, who met her on an aero-engineering course at Chatham, taught her to jump and took her on demonstration tours of Scandinavia, the Continent, and America, using the 'Guardian Angel'.

In 1919 Sylva made what was thought to be the first jump in

Britain by a woman from a plane in flight, when she parachuted from a Handley Page biplane during a display at Cricklewood, North London. Eighteen months later she made a dare-devil, if not foolhardy, jump from a German aircraft travelling at 160 m.p.h. into a wind registering 60 m.p.h. at ground level. No modern jumper would sensibly attempt such a feat, which would be bound to result in a dangerously swinging descent and a violent landing. But to everyone's surprise, Sylva survived.

Lacking the momentum of war to carry them on, most nations let parachute research fall into abeyance. In Britain, Calthrop's was still regarded as the best parachute we had, though not officially adopted, and in May of 1919 it enjoyed one brief hour of public glory. A Handley Page bomber zoomed in over Hyde Park and dropped by parachute a bouquet of roses, which were hastened by car to Marlborough House as a gift for Queen Alexandra.

In the United States, Britain's languid lack of interest in the parachute idea was not shared—at least, not by the Army, which was anxious to develop its Air Corps and conserve, through safety, the huge investment which it made in each trainee. Ideas began to take physical shape late in 1918. The U.S. Army earmarked funds for parachute development and in an old aircraft hangar at the McCook Flying Field, Dayton, Ohio, the work went ahead.

Major E. L. Hoffman, an aeronautical engineer, who took charge as military leader, quickly gathered around him a small team of zealots, including a veteran pilot, Floyd Smith, a brilliant technician who in 1910 had built his own aircraft and in 1914, as the result of a near-fatal air accident, had been toying with the idea of a manually operated parachute pack. As the war progressed and the need for parachutes became manifest, Smith became a dedicated enthusiast, and willingly joined the team from his job in aircraft production engineering with the Army Air Service.

His companions in the McCook team were Guy Ball, a former racing driver, James M. Russell (later famous for his 'Lobe' parachute), Jimmy Higgins, a former car salesman, and Sergeant

Ralph Bottriell, an army balloonist and parachutist. Although most of them had no experience whatever in parachute design, they generated tremendous energy. At McCook the modern parachute was born.

Hoffman busied himself with a programme of dummy drops with existing parachutes garnered from all over the world, among them the 'Guardian Angel' and the Mears from Britain, the Heinecke from Germany, the French S.T.A., made of cotton, the American A.E.F., and the French Robert.

Rigorous tests, conducted under all types of conditions, ultimately led to one incontrovertible conclusion: that the attached-type parachute was inadequate for aircraft emergency use and should be abandoned. Apart from its bulk and discomfort, too much could go wrong: shroud lines could become entangled, canopies were too weak to withstand air pressure during deployment at high speed. Even under first-class conditions they proved unreliable and were consistently fouled by aircraft.

So the McCook team drew up a list of stringent requirements which their ideal parachute should meet:

1. The parachute must make it possible for the airman to leave the aircraft regardless of the position it might be in when disabled.

2. The operating means must not depend on the airman falling from the aircraft.

3. The parachute equipment must be fastened to the body of the airman at all times while he is in the aircraft.

4. Operating the parachute must not be complicated; it must not be liable to foul or be susceptible to damage from any ordinary service conditions.

5. The parachute must be of such a size and be so disposed to give the maximum comfort to the wearer and allow him to leave the aircraft with the least possible difficulty or delay.

6. It must open promptly and be capable of withstanding the shock of a 200 pound load falling at 400 m.p.h.

7. It must be reasonably steerable.

8. The harness must be comfortable and very strong, and designed so as to transfer the shock of opening without physical injury to the airman. It must be sufficiently adjustable to fit large and small people.

9. The harness must prevent the airman from falling out when the parachute opens, and it must be possible for him to remove it quickly when landing in water or a high wind.

10. The strength of the 'follow through' must be uniform to the top of the parachute.

11. The parachute must be simple in construction and be easily packed with little time and labour.

Painstakingly, Hoffman, Russell, Smith, Ball, and a newcomer to the team, Leslie Leroy Irvin, picked their way through the problems towards a hundred-per-cent free-fall parachute. They experimented with canopies, ranging in diameter between 20 feet and 34 feet, shaped the panels, and used a tough grade of silk that would stand up to increasing aircraft speeds. Into the apex they put a yard-diameter flexible vent to soften the shock of opening and relieve the air pressure during deployment. They improved harnesses, using strong webbing, substituted braided silk rigging lines for hemp to make them more flexible and free of the tendency to twist.

The result was the 'A' type free-fall pack parachute. Pack flaps were flipped open by a system of elastic cords operated by a hand-operated ripcord, and a small auxiliary parachute, two feet in diameter, made the opening even more positive. The pilot or auxiliary 'chute sat on the main one above the vent, with its own tiny rigging lines connecting to the parent and braced with steel ribs and powerful springs.

Floyd Smith applied for a patent for such a parachute on July 27, 1918, and the patent was granted on May 18, 1920. The ripcord was attached to a ring on the wearer's chest, and also to thread ties on the back pack.

The parachute showed up well in dummy tests and in April 1919 Major Hoffman decided it was time to try a live drop, never before attempted with his free-fall parachute. The man chosen to make it was Irvin, to whom scores of thousands of airmen in Britain, the United States and indeed the world over were, in years to come, to owe their survival.

Irvin, a short, well-built young man in his mid-twenties, was a parachute engineer with a varied but curiously single-minded background. Exactly how he reached the parachute 'laboratory' at McCook Field is uncertain, for accounts vary in detail. It seems that Major Hoffman, hearing of Irvin's interest and experience in the parachute field, invited him by letter to help in their researches. When Irvin first went along, he had with him an attached-type parachute of his own design, but was told that this system had been ruled out in favour of the free-fall, ripcord type. Thereupon, he and Floyd Smith joined forces, and it was largely due to their efforts that the Type 'A' prototype was produced.

Even as a boy, Irvin had been fascinated by parachutes. He was a keen spectator at local carnivals, watching enthralled at jumps from hot-air balloons in his home town, Los Angeles. One of his early exploits as a schoolboy was to make a large model balloon-and-parachute with a release mechanism that he had worked out himself. To the parachute, beneath the balloon, he attached a cat, which he sent soaring high over Los Angeles. Unfortunately for the cat, the release mechanism failed to work, and it, and the model balloon, were wafted out to sea never to return. The experience worked one resolve on the chastened Irvin: never again would he involve anyone but himself in his own experiments.

Having left school at fourteen, Irvin went to work for an aeroplane inventor, became an assistant to a stunt car driver (acting as ballast on fast corners!), then balloonist with Universal Films and a high diver at circuses. It was his experience in the last role, leaping into a net, that convinced him that falling did not, as was widely supposed, cause a man to lose consciousness or control.

At the age of sixteen he persuaded a circus proprietor to let him stand in for an umbrella jumper, Captain Campbell, who had to abandon his act because of illness. Receiving his father's permission, Irvin did so, and stayed with the circus three years. As time went on he increased the size of the jump, and the umbrella. Eventually, he was experimenting with parachutes and, billed as 'Ski-Hi Irvin', was soon performing balloon drops throughout his home state of California. Later, though it took a 'sweetener' to persuade the pilot to take him up, Irvin made a jump from an aircraft with a parachute stuffed in a sack under the cockpit—one of the earliest jumps ever made from a plane. It was an attached-type 'chute: a manually operated one was still an unrealised dream.

During World War I, Irvin worked for the Curtiss Aeroplane Co. at Buffalo, New York, spending much of his time designing and making his parachute. When completed, the prototype was about 32 feet in diameter, had 24 silk rigging lines and a $2\frac{1}{2}$-feet-diameter pilot parachute. Late in 1918 he tried it out repeatedly with a life-sized dummy from a Curtiss plane, attaching a static line to tug the ripcord as it fell. It fell to earth safely every time.

But when he took it along to McCook Field, it was of course found to fall short of several of the requirements listed by the team, and was therefore ruled out.

Later, Irvin and Smith produced the free-fall Type 'A', which was smaller than Irvin's in diameter (about 28 feet) but was similar in other respects. However, it successfully managed to run the gauntlet of the team's list of eleven essentials.

Irvin was now twenty-four and married, with a young child. On April 19, 1919, while his young wife Velda waited apprehensively at their Los Angeles home with his three-year-old daughter, Irvin was to make history at McCook Field, by jumping from a DH-4 biplane.

He carried his parachute on his back, with a harness specially designed to brace his whole body so as to spread the shock of opening; over his shoulders went the webbing, round his waist, under his legs and up the front of his body, with connector hooks at chest and thighs. He carried a second parachute as a reserve; this was a concession to pessimists who were convinced that a ripcord type parachute would fail, but Irvin was equally convinced that it wouldn't.

Floyd Smith, the pilot, took the DH up to 1,500 feet and came in smoothly for a level run at 100 m.p.h. Irvin gave Smith a farewell wave and vanished over the side, snatching the ripcord as he fell. By the time he had dropped 1,000 feet, the parachute was full-blown, and he floated down with only one mishap to mar the fall. In his excitement he landed badly, and broke an ankle. What he had *not* done, as many feared he would, was break his neck; nor had he become unconscious. More positively, the success of the manually operated parachute now seemed assured. In the following weeks many more jumps were made, and the U.S. Army, satisfied with the results, then turned to the matter of contracts. In June 1919 Irvin was given his first order for 300 parachutes, and found he had now become a parachute-manufacturer and business man.

A month later occurred the first major disaster involving attached-type parachutes, though they were not the cause. On July 21 the dirigible 'Wing Foot Express', built principally to publicise the rubber company which owned it, set off on a test flight over Chicago, carrying a pilot, John A. Boettner, mechanics Henry Wacker and Buck Weaver, Earl Davenport (a publicity man) and Milton G. Norton, a press photographer.

At five in the afternoon, about 1,200 feet up, the dirigible suddenly buckled in half in a huge mass of flame. All in the blimp except Davenport jumped with their parachutes, but only three survived. Weaver's 'chute was immediately burnt to a fragment by the wreckage, and he fell to his death on nothing but rigging lines. Wacker's parachute caught fire too, but the rush of air as he descended snuffed out the flames. Boettner's began to burn, but he landed before it properly caught fire, and Norton, who started down well, landed up against a building and fell to the street, fatally injured.

The wreckage of the blimp wrought dreadful havoc. It sank down on a large bank building, its engine and fuel tank smashing through into a section where girl typists and filing clerks worked.

All told, the disaster killed thirteen people, and injured thirty others. And despite an inquiry, the cause of the fire remained a mystery.

Although the McCook team were happy with the new ripcord parachute, they continued to experiment with static line models if only to prove that they had exhausted every possibility. It was during these experiments that a young RAF officer from England, Lieut. R. A. Caldwell, helped in a tragic way to vindicate their scepticism.

Caldwell had gone out to McCook with Major Orde-Lees to demonstrate the 'Guardian Angel'. On the day of the jump the parachute was fixed as usual beneath the fuselage, the attachment rope snaking up to Caldwell in one of the cockpits. The plane soared to about 900 feet, and then he jumped. It was a horrifying experience not only for Caldwell, but for those watching below: for poor Caldwell could be seen dangling helplessly beneath the plane, his life-line hooked up on an elevator rocker arm. In seconds it was cut through and Caldwell, trailing frayed rope, plummeted to earth and in five seconds was dead. As far as the Americans were concerned, hopes for the attached-type parachute died with him.

During later tests on other parachutes, an incident occurred that gave Irvin immense satisfaction. In August 1920, Mr LeRoy B. Jahn, a fellow American, went along to demonstrate his new quick-opening parachute, which incorporated four enormous springs, each about four feet long. These were stitched into the parachute's skirt or periphery, to help deployment, and they were compressed to about a foot long when packed. After slightly modifying the design, Jahn sought to prove its reliability from a plane, using an employee, William O'Connor, as the jumper.

With the memory of Caldwell's fatal drop still sickeningly fresh, the McCook men were disinclined to take any more chances; they insisted on Jahn's man carrying a standard Irvin in reserve. Jahn took great exception to this, accusing them of insulting his own parachute. But the Army was firm: the Irvin in addition or no demonstration. Reluctantly, O'Connor donned the

Irvin as well as the Jahn, and jumped from 2,000 feet. For 1,500 feet he dropped like lead, his Jahn parachute flapping uselessly above his head, entangled with the giant springs. Quickly, O'Connor pulled the ripcord of the Irvin—and landed alive.

But it was to be another two years before a pilot used Irvin's parachute in an emergency. By this time, after more than 50,000 test jumps, the Army Air Corps had made the wearing of parachutes compulsory. The decision was inspired by the death of one Lieut. F. W. Niedermeyer, who one day forgot to put on the parachute he customarily wore. He was taking part in combat practice with a friend when his plane collapsed in mid-air, throwing him out from sufficient height to kill him.

Seven months later, Lieut. Harold H. Harris, an experienced pilot, was flying a Loening plane to continue tests with partly balanced ailerons. The aircraft had been flown the previous day and given no trouble. As he flew over Dayton, Ohio, he spotted another plane flown by a Lieut. Fairchild, and both began air fighting practice. During this 'bout' Harris lost control of the plane, which began to dive at such a speed that chunks of wing fell off. Realising the plane was doomed, Harris unclipped his safety belt, stood up and was swept up and out of the cockpit.

As he spun down he pulled what he thought was the ripcord of the parachute. To his dismay, nothing happened. Three times he tugged away with the same result. Then he realised that what he had been pulling was part of his leg harness. After 1,800 feet of free fall, he found the ripcord ring and the parachute opened at about 700 feet from the ground. It was his first jump ever—and the first real aircraft emergency drop to have been made with the Irvin.

(*Above left*) Paratroops pock-mark the sky over Arnhem
in 1944 – a photograph taken from a transport aircraft.
(*Below*) WAAF parachute packers during the Second World War.
(*Above right*) Parachutes in clusters, for stability, were used then
as now for dropping heavy supplies, such as armoured vehicles.

The famous picture of a Lightning jet pilot's parachute opening as his ejection seat hurls him clear of his diving plane. The ejection seat was developed during the Second World War by Sir James Martin (*left*), now managing director of the Martin-Baker Aircraft Company. (This picture is from a painting by Howard Barron.)

8

PARACHUTES FOR ALL

In England in the early 1920s, Calthrop was still making little headway with the 'Guardian Angel', though he continued to have an influential and forceful ally in Major Orde-Lees. In February 1920, in the pages of *Flight* magazine, Orde-Lees took issue with Colonel H. E. S. Holt, who had invented a free-fall parachute. Holt's other devices included a flare dispenser, an acetylene burner to help aircraft to land, a gadget for dropping mailbags from aircraft and a suit for pilots with large pockets to house his parachute and its auxiliary, which were released with a timing device.

Holt's free-fall parachute was similar to many being marketed in the United States. He claimed that it was much safer than attached-type parachutes because it would be more likely to open when a plane was diving steeply and when the differences in speeds between the jumper and the aircraft might not be sufficient to tug an attached-type parachute from its housing on the plane. Col. Holt's free-fall 'chute was being studied at the RAF's experimental station at Orfordness, but he criticised the RAF parachute section for being 'obsessed' with trying to find a parachute system which would function when used from a plane flying normally, under control. 'But then,' he asked, 'who wants to escape from a machine flying normally, under control?' The automatic type, like the 'Guardian Angel', no doubt functioned beautifully under ordinary conditions, said the colonel, but it was a deathtrap if used from a machine which had crumpled in mid-air—unless the pilot fell faster than the machine so that he could haul the parachute out.

Orde-Lees, in a lengthy piece of special pleading for the 'Guardian Angel', argued that when he used an attached-type his pulse rate shot up from 56 to 112, but with what he called a 'problematical' opener i.e. a ripcord 'chute, it went up even farther—to 129. 'Let any of the positive-opening-no-use experts come forward and jump from any low height,' he wrote, 'and I'll undertake (because I've done it already) to go one lower in altitude every time with a positive-opener. No dummies, please.'

In Parliament, the abortive question-and-answer game went on. In May 1919 the Air Ministry was urged to amend the Civil Air Regulations and make parachutes compulsory. The Air Ministry spokesman, Major-General J. E. B. Seely, said predictably, that the question was receiving 'close attention', but 'development has not at present reached the stage in which compulsory universal provision would be either practical or advantageous for military or civil aviation'. A little later, Mr Baldwin Raper, M.P., a former war pilot, tried his 15-stone weight on a 'Guardian Angel' from a Handley Page at 600 feet to get first-hand information of the value and efficiency of parachutes. The 'Guardian Angel' was efficient enough to let him down lightly.

It was Mr Raper who elicited the interesting information in Parliament in July 1921 that the RAF then had 1,943 parachutes. Fitting, it surprised nobody to hear, had been delayed because of difficulties over harness design. A few planes and one balloon were equipped: 'Experiments are proceeding and satisfactory results are expected shortly.'

The early 1920s were depressing years for parachute advocates. In August 1921 they lost one of the most devoted workers in the cause of air safety, former president of the parachute committee and the first man to parachute from an airship in flight, Air Commodore Maitland. Ironically, Maitland was killed in an airship disaster, when forty-four people out of a total of forty-nine were killed in the R.38.

One of the five survivors was Mr Harry Bateman of the National Physical Laboratory, who said the suddenness of the disaster prevented the general use of parachutes. Only seconds elapsed between the airship's buckling and its dive into the River Humber.

The following year, parachute pioneer William Newell was killed by his own trivial neglect. Surprisingly, for so experienced a jumper, Newell failed to make an essential adjustment to his parachute before a jump made during a visit to Copenhagen, and as a result, part of the canopy remained lodged in the container. The aircraft pilot flew down to 60 feet over water, so that Newell could release himself and fall without injury. Newell certainly dropped, but drowned after suffering from cold and exhaustion, having swum only 20 yards.

Meanwhile, Britain's airmen were still without parachutes, and Captain Frederick Guest, the Air Secretary, announced in the Commons that no fighting aircraft were fitted with them. No practice or experimental drops were being permitted from heavier-than-air craft, though 140 parachutes had been issued for Avro trainers, and the need for any modifications and improvements would be reported on.

The position was thus practically stagnant. Rumours spread that the parachute research department was being depleted, and officers were said to be leaving. Was this true? asked Sir William Joynson Hicks in the Commons. 'I hope not,' replied Capt. Guest, and hastened away to find out. A week later he wrote to Sir William admitting that the separate research section had indeed closed down—in the interests of economy. There was no intention to abandon research on parachutes, he said; this would be carried out by another department.

If research *did* continue, it led nowhere at all. It was three years before Capt. Guest's successor, Sir Samuel Hoare, made the long-awaited, long overdue announcement about parachute provision. The question of air safety appliances was now so urgent, he told M.P.s, in March 1925, that they could wait no longer for a satisfactory type to be produced in Britain. Therefore the RAF would henceforth be equipped with the parachute made by Leslie Irvin in the United States. Two-thirds of the initial order of 2,261 would be imported; the balance, and all future supplies, would be made in Britain. Irvin came to England and in 1926 founded his factory at Letchworth, Hertfordshire, where it flourishes to this day.

This sudden development was no doubt a blow to Col. Holt, whose 'Autochute' resembled the Irvin in many respects. He had demonstrated an early version as much as seven years before, and an up-to-date version not long after the decision to equip the RAF with the Irvin—a parachute which he claimed had embodied several features that he had previously abandoned. But the telling factor in favour of the Irvin was its proven value in the United States after 1918.

The 'Autochute' was a seat-pack ripcord type, like the Irvin, and it had a pilot 'chute, also like the Irvin, which was released either by the pilot himself or automatically. Some 'Autochute' models had a third 'chute between the pilot and the main canopy to reduce the shock of opening. The rigging lines were ingeniously stored in silk tubes to prevent entanglement. It was demonstrated at Stag Lane aerodrome in November 1925 by Capt. H. Spencer, a parachutist who had made over a hundred drops. He dived from a D.H.9 head first at 1,000 feet and made a perfect landing.

More than anyone, though, the introduction of the Irvin in Britain hit Everard Calthrop, who had invested so much money, energy, patriotism and sheer compassion for the risk-ridden wartime pilots in his attached-type 'Guardian Angel'. He died in 1927, a disappointed man. The only rewards for his years of dogged effort were two honours from the Italian Government (the 'Guardian Angel' had been used with distinction on the Italian front in World War I) and a will worth £1,777. In the same year, Major Hoffman, of McCook Field, U.S.A., received the important Collier Trophy for 'the most distinguished contribution to the science of flight' for his work to perfect a free-fall parachute.

One of Hoffman's team, it will be recalled, was James M. Russell, who devised two interesting parachutes, one of which competed for Government approval in England. Russell, after being asked by Hoffman to make a parachute providing 'positive opening', produced the Valve, which had been patented in 1924. It had no vent in the apex, but instead featured valve-like openings in the overlapping parts of the panels. For various reasons the

Valve was never used, but it led Russell to design another and more important model, the uniquely shaped 'Lobe'.

Russell recognised that the development of the parachute had been concentrated on the pack, harness and method of attachment or deployment; the canopy itself had changed little fundamentally from the mushroom it had always been. Even the Irvin maintained this tradition.

Russell claimed that both the spring in the Irvin pilot parachute and the elastic in the pack which hastened its opening were affected by climatic conditions, and required re-packing. Moreover, he felt, the pilot 'chute might foul and not pull the main parachute from the pack; shroud lines might become twisted; and below 200 feet, performance was variable.

With the 'Lobe', Russell hoped to overcome the principal weakness of other parachutes, including the Valve—namely, a tendency to oscillate, the curse of parachute jumping since Garnerin's day. His answer was to dispense with the pilot 'chute, flatten the canopy and turn the edge under in a wide curve. Oscillation almost disappeared, and he also achieved a quicker opening by enabling it to do so horizontally by means of modifications to the pack.

The new 'Lobe' parachute created no small stir when it was tested in 1927. The shock on opening was a mere one-third of that of other parachutes, but one problem remained—a tendency for the shroud lines to hook over the canopy when it opened. Two young test jumpers cured this by a continuous and dangerous process of trial and error, leaping in such a way as to foul the parachute deliberately. When the back pack was improved, the trouble stopped.

During the 1920s, Russell was joined as demonstrator by John Tranum, a Danish-born stunt man whose repertoire included such feats as playing tennis with a partner on the wing of a plane in flight, wing-walking, and transferring from one aircraft to another in mid-flight. Tranum visited England with the object of helping to set up a factory for Russell, to be built with American capital, but using British labour to man it. On one occasion

Tranum met Calthrop and negotiated supplies of fabric. Tranum's view of Calthrop was patronising: he thought Calthrop's 'Guardian Angel' factory was well organised, but thought little of his parachute—a typical product of a railway engineer, in his disparaging opinion.

Russell's 'Lobe' was intended primarily for commercial use, but Tranum tried hard to catch the interest of the Air Ministry. They liked the 'Lobe' but considered it no better than the Irvin they had adopted, and saw no reason to change.

John Tranum was one of the greatest exponents of stunt jumping of all time. He was utterly fearless, and fully lived up to his confident visiting-card slogan, 'Aerial stunts to order'. Tranum was one of a large corps of aerial acrobats who proliferated in postwar America, many of them World War I pilots whose only skill, flying, was not enough to guarantee them other work. So they bought up hundreds of redundant war planes and set the United States buzzing in the only way they knew.

Tranum's introduction to parachuting came about one day when the scheduled jumper at a display failed to turn up. He was offered fifty dollars to make a jump, asked for sixty and got it. One of his early film exploits was to leap from a burning Nieuport into the wings of which ground staff had squirted gallons of petrol. It was set on fire at 7,000 feet and Tranum parachuted down to a useful 200 dollars.

But he was sensitive, too, to the more aesthetic delights of parachute jumping—the silent aerial solitude, with only a gentle distant murmur of activity to remind him that life was going on below. 'What a grand and glorious feeling' he wrote in *Nine Lives*.[1] 'Here I was, all by myself, the machine going on in the distance above, below me hundreds of people like so many flies, all looking up. I marvelled at the wonderful stillness around me, only faint noises from the ground were reaching me, such as cows bellowing, dogs barking, and the roar of excitement from the crowd, and I cascading down through golden sunshine on a long, regular slant towards earth.'

[1] John Hamilton, 1933.

But stunting was his forte, and in this he led the field for years. One of his jumps was from Pasadena Bridge, in California, which, like the higher span of Tower Bridge, lies 154 feet above the river. When Major Orde-Lees jumped into the Thames he was using the attached-type parachute, the 'Guardian Angel', but Tranum used a ripcord type already opened out, and dived in off the top of his parked car. On another occasion, for a film company, he drove a motor-cycle with a parachute attached to it over a cliff. As soon as it was airborne he opened the parachute, let the motor-cycle crash, and landed unharmed into a 1,000 feet deep canyon below.

One day Tranum made an attempt to upstage a stunter named Simpson whose personal speciality was a long drop of 1,000 or 2,000 feet before letting out his parachute, which he held in his arms. Simpson's big mistake was to assume that the current of air would necessarily be upwards; when he threw out the canopy, it was blown against him and he dropped from 6,000 feet to within a few hundred feet of the ground before the parachute, which, wrapping itself round him had almost become his shroud, blew open.

Tranum's reply to this was to play with the idea that killed the unfortunate Cocking nearly a century before. Tranum used an ordinary non-rigid parachute, attached a cord to the apex inside the canopy and then hauled it down so as to convert it almost into an inverted cone. The effect, as he pulled on the cord, was to reduce the drag and speed up his descent, and only when he approached the ground did he let go the central cord and slow himself to a safe speed.

Tranum also specialised in delayed drops, timing his free-fall with a stopwatch as he went. It was during the prelude to one of these attempts that he died. In March 1935, after an astonishing lifetime of tempting a merciful Providence, Tranum was taken up in a plane from Kastrup airport in Denmark, with the object of dropping 25,000 feet to break his own 17,250 feet free-fall record. During the flight, Tranum suddenly slumped in his seat. The pilot took the plane down immediately, and doctors spent hours trying to bring Tranum round. But in vain. He had died of a heart attack

—not at all the spectacular sort of death he might have chosen for himself.

The stunt jumpers, like their nineteenth-century forerunners, may have performed mainly for the thrills, and been thrilling to watch, but their apparently pointless work did contain, indirectly, some long-term benefits to aviation. Parachute experts who watched their antics learned something of the limits of human endurance in the air, and thus about what could be expected of the parachute and the man. The myth that the speed of a free-fall descent would send a man unconscious had already been exploded by Irvin and others, and it had been established also that, far from a man falling at 250 m.p.h., as widely thought, the maximum speed he would fall at would be little more than 120 m.p.h. under normal conditions.

One of the dare-devils of the time was Charles A. Lindbergh, who became the first man to make a solo nonstop flight across the Atlantic at the age of twenty-five when he flew from Long Island to Paris in May 1927. Lindbergh learned to fly after World War I, and for a time toured the United States barnstorming with exhibition jumps.

Four times he was to save his life by Irvin parachute. The first occasion was in 1924 when he joined the U.S. Army. He had his first taste of danger at Kelly Field, Texas, while taking part in a mock attack on a bomber. Lindbergh, in company with another plane, piloted by a Lieut. McCallister in the top unit of a formation of nine S.E.5s, was converging on a DH 4B at about 5,000 feet. He recounted what ensued in an official report, quoted in his book *We—Pilot and Plane*.[1]

I passed above the DH and a moment later felt a slight jolt. My head was thrown forward against the cowling and my plane seemed to turn around and hang nearly motionless for an instant. I closed the throttle and saw an S.E.5 with Lieut. McCallister in the cockpit a few feet away on my left. He was apparently unhurt and getting ready to jump.

[1] G. P. Putnam's Sons, 1927.

Our ships were locked together with fuselages approximately parallel. My right wing was damaged and folded back slightly, covering the forward right hand corner of his cockpit. Then the ships started to mill around and the wires began whistling. The right wing started vibrating and striking my head at the bottom of each oscillation. I removed the rubber band safe-tying the belt, unbuckled it, climbed out past the trailing edge of the damaged wing and with my feet on the cowling on the right side of the cockpit, which was then in a nearly vertical position, I jumped backward as far from the ship as possible.

I had no difficulty in locating the pull-ring and experienced no sensation of falling. The wreckage was falling nearly straight down and for some time I fell in line with its path. Fearing the wreckage might fall on me, I did not pull the ripcord until I had dropped several hundred feet into the clouds.

During this time I had turned one-half revolution and was falling flat and nearly face downwards. The parachute functioned perfectly; almost as soon as I pulled the ripcord, the riser jerked on my shoulders, the straps tightened, my head went down and the chute was fully opened.

I saw Lieut. McCallister floating above me and the wrecked ships about 100 yards to one side, continuing to spin to the right and leaving a trail of lighter fragments along their path. I watched them until, still locked together, they crashed . . . about 2,000 feet below and burst into flames several seconds after impact.

McCallister came down safely, and Lindbergh landed unhurt on the edge of a ditch, after losing his goggles, a camera and the rip-cord of the parachute.

He made his second parachute escape when he took a new aircraft up for testing. He had not intended to wear a 'chute at all, but the duty officer of the day had insisted, and within ten minutes Lindbergh had abundant cause for thanks. He put his plane into a spin at 2,500 feet and could not pull out. So he jumped, at a mere 300, and was fortunate enough to survive.

His third and fourth escapes were in 1926, after he had become an Air Mail pilot. On the first occasion, he found himself in fog while flying at night between St Louis and Chicago, with his petrol running out rapidly. He baled out 'blind' at 5,000 feet, with a flashlamp in his belt. Soon after he jumped he heard the engine of his plane start up again very near his descending parachute. The plane shot past him and crashed two miles away.

Two months later, Lindbergh jumped for the last time, this time at a record 13,000 feet, in snow. He finished up on a barbed wire fence, but apart from scratches suffered no injury. Later he flew out to collect the mail bag, which had dropped undamaged, and flew it back.

Lindbergh was the first member of Irvin's Caterpillar Club, an exclusive association of airmen who had made a successful emergency jump using an Irvin parachute, to have undertaken four life-saving descents. The first emergency jump made with an Irvin parachute was by Lieut. Harold Harris of the U.S. Army Air Service over Dayton, Ohio, in 1922, and he became Caterpillar Number One as a result. His reward was a small gold caterpillar pin and a certificate signed personally by Leslie Irvin (a similar pin is presented to each Caterpillar even today, but the certificates are signed by Irvin's widow, who lives in Los Angeles). The caterpillar or silkworm device was chosen by Irvin a few days after Harris's jump, because it symbolised life hanging by a thread from the silken canopy of the parachute.

Lindbergh's tally of four emergency jumps was, however, not unique: it was equalled some years later—in the Battle of Britain,

9

PRELUDE TO WAR

IT WAS not long before the advantages of the ripcord parachute became clear even to firm believers in the old attached-type. In May 1925, shortly after the Air Ministry had approved the Irvin and decided to adopt it for the RAF, Major Orde-Lees, doughty campaigner for the 'Guardian Angel', publicly turned his coat.

He wrote in *The Times* that he himself would have recommended this type for pilots. 'Long experience has brought me gradually to the conclusion that [the free-fall type] is likely to save more lives in the long run owing to its freedom from any possibility of fouling the machine, provided that the ripcord of the knapsack in which it is contained is not pulled too soon. . .

'Parachutes will not save every life, of course, but they will give us a sporting chance which we never had before. During the war a high percentage of German aviators were saved by their parachutes. We sacrificed about 8,000[1] lives for want of parachutes. At least 4,000 of those aviators could have been saved.'

What Calthrop's feelings were can only be conjectured, but not everyone felt as Orde-Lees did. Opponents of the free-fall concept felt vindicated the same month when a young airman, Corporal Sydney Wilson, of No. 12 Squadron RAF, lost his nerve in a first-time jump and failed to use either the main or reserve parachute and was killed. There, admonished the anti-free-fall school, that is what happens when you place too great an onus on a jumper—such as having to pull the ripcord. Consternation by the public led to questions in the Commons and for a time scepticism was renewed.

An accident involving a civilian the following year emphasised the lethal consequences of lack of parachute training or sound

[1] An exaggeration: the true figure, according to the official history, *War in the Air*, by H. A. Jones (O.U.P., 1937) is 6,166.—J.L.

equipment, and led to an Air Ministry regulation aimed specifically at civilians. At Leicester on September 9, an aircraft pilot, Capt. A. F. Muir, who had been giving exhibition flights, conducting passenger trips and organising parachute descents, took up a would-be jumper, 25-year-old Mrs Dorothy Cain.

Earlier in the week several trouble-free jumps had been made with an attached-type parachute—the one being used by Mrs Cain. Having fitted on her harness, the pilot flew her up to 1,000 feet and signalled her to jump. The crowd of 40,000 below saw Mrs Cain emerge from the plane and leap into space. Immediately came the agonising realisation that she had no parachute. Somehow it had become detached from her body and could be seen trailing from its case beneath the fuselage. Her distant figure, spreadeagled as it swam through space, thudded to earth and she was killed instantly—and before the eyes of her husband in the crowd. For several days he had tried to convince her that it was unwise to jump at all.

Four days after the tragedy, the Air Ministry reacted with a ban on descents from civil aircraft unless permitted by directions issued by the Secretary of State. Applications to make a jump had to be made 14 days in advance.

Parachutes were soon compulsory in the French air force; in the RAF airmen were being trained in their use. They had to be able to pack their parachutes before they made practice jumps.

From 1926 onwards all new British aircraft were designed to accommodate seat pack parachutes. A parachute training unit was formed at Henlow, Bedfordshire, and here young airmen were schooled in jumping first with a couple of 'pull off' falls from a Vickers Vimy at about 500 feet. This meant standing on a specially built platform on one of the bracing struts between the wings, pulling the parachute ripcord and letting the wind fill out the canopy. The 'pull off' invariably followed, and in any struggle for second thoughts the parachute always won. Later, there followed a free-fall jump from about 3,000 feet.

Parachutes became compulsory for aircraft test pilots too. One of the side benefits of this was that testing could be pushed to the limits of performance without serious risk to life. In Copenhagen, for example, a pilot commissioned to discover the cause of a Fokker's break-up in mid-air, put his machine into a steep dive at 9,000 feet and, when the wings broke up, jumped to safety before the machine crashed.

Attempts were made in Britain on behalf of various parachute types, such as the Russell 'Lobe', to interest the Services, but without success. One candidate was an Italian parachute, the Salvator, which had been invented by an Italian officer and adopted by his country's air force. The Salvator could be used either with a static line, or as a free type by operating a hand grip on the belt instead of a ripcord. It had an excellent safety record, and demonstrations at Hendon impressed British officials. But again, the Irvin had pre-empted it. Later, the Salvator was adopted by air forces in Japan, Spain and Switzerland.

General Guidoni, the former Italian Air Attaché in London, was killed when experimenting with the Salvator, though the parachute could hardly be blamed for it. During a test at 3,000 feet, the general pulled the belt lever and jumped simultaneously without ensuring he was clear of the aircraft. The rigging lines became tangled and the canopy did not deploy.

By the end of 1928, the Irvin was becoming widely popular. It was being used in twenty-seven countries, and at Letchworth production had reached thirty-five parachutes a week, all for the RAF, compared with fifty a week by the parent company in Buffalo. At Letchworth, Leslie Irvin gave his employees a useful lesson, when one of his demonstrators jumped from a D.H. monoplane piloted by Irvin himself. Seeing a parachute in action was a new experience for most of them, though they had been making the RAF's parachutes for two years.

By the end of 1930, the Fleet Air Arm was equipped throughout with the Irvin quick release parachute, whose central fitting was turned 90 degrees and allowed four attachment points to disengage simultaneously so that pilots could get free in water. Several other types of parachute were now available, including a 'form fitting' pack for use in aircraft cabins which slipped into the shape of the upholstery. But the seat pack remained standard. At that time Irvin calculated that two lives were being saved for every hundred parachutes sold; so far 20,000 of their parachutes had been made and used.

Jumps were being made from greater and greater altitudes . . . 16,000, 18,000 and then 24,000 feet by a German airwoman, Frau Schröter in 1932. Such feats attracted considerable public interest —far more than the fact that enthusiasm for parachuting had quickened in Russia. A mere hundred jumps were made there in 1930, 600 in 1931 and 2,000 in 1932. Within the next three years 1,300 parachute clubs and more than a hundred centres had sprung up, well-equipped and provided with training towers.

As far back as 1927 the Russians had dropped eight men behind the 'enemy' lines during manoeuvres. In similar exercises in the 1930s, Russian troops swung down by parachute in their thousands, impressing such senior British officers as Major-General (later Field Marshal) Archibald Wavell, but not sufficiently to call for paratroop units in Britain.

The Russians also went in for delayed drops. In 1937 Lieut. Kaytanov, an air force officer, was flown up to 36,000 feet. He jumped and dropped to 4,000 before he opened his parachute—a world record at the time.

In England, a new personality began to appear on the parachute scene who was to have an indirect but profound effect on warfare in 1939–45—Raymond Quilter, a former Guards officer, and a keen amateur flier, who flew his own plane at Brooklands, as well as parachutist. He was the son of a rich Suffolk baronet, Sir Cuthbert Quilter.

Quilter junior had a restless, questing mind and was seldom satisfied with the status quo. Like Irvin, who had by now settled in England and with whom he later became a warm personal friend, Quilter liked the gay life. After a while these pleasures began to pall, and he sought other outlets for his energy. Around 1930, Quilter encountered James Gregory, an extrovert enthusiast with a considerable parachute background. Gregory had started as a member of the first parachute section of the RAF in 1919, later becoming works manager for Calthrop at his 'Guardian Angel' factory, and then for the Russell Parachute Company, makers of the 'Lobe'.

The parachutes currently used, claimed Quilter and Gregory, were capable of a good deal of improvement, so they decided to make their own. Money was no great problem. Arthur Dickinson, who was financial adviser to Sir Cuthbert, managed to persuade him to put up money for his son to buy silk fabric for parachutes, and Dickinson joined the group to watch his client's interests.

The first few experimental emergency parachutes were made by Gregory and his wife on a sewing machine at home. By 1932, from these small beginnings, Quilter and Gregory had designed a parachute to Air Ministry specifications, and cheap enough to be within easy reach of the private flier's pocket. It had a quick-acting pilot parachute, and the pack was padded with sorbo for comfort.

They were beginning to find lack of working space a serious hindrance until Reginald Dagnall came to their aid. Owner of the RFD company which made, among other items, flotation gear to buoy up the wings of aircraft forced to land at sea, Dagnall was impressed by the Gregory-Quilter team enough to offer them a corner of his works in Guildford, and to loan machinery. In 1934 the GQ Company was formed, with Quilter, Dickinson and Dagnall as its first directors.

The company aimed high from the start: they would compete with Irvin on his own ground and sell parachutes to the RAF, cash in on the commercial aviation boom by providing a parachute for every passenger, and sell parachutes to the moneyed young fliers who droned the weekends away over Brooklands.

It was a prosperous dream: the reality was different. Although GQ were allowed to tender to the Air Ministry, they were repeatedly rebuffed when it came to the point of actual orders. The Ministry could see no reason to disturb the exclusivity they had granted to Irvin.

Nor were the civil airlines interested in their parachutes, on several grounds: parachutes would increase a plane's weight;

women would need to wear slacks to accommodate the harness, thus detracting from what was then regarded largely as a social event; and suggesting that a plane might crash by urging passengers to wear parachutes was a psychological deterrent. Moreover, with the increase in trans-Channel and transatlantic flying, the airlines did not want passengers throwing themselves into water. They would rather have them come down with the plane on the sea, where flotation gear would keep it buoyant till rescue came.

There was also the key fact that air accidents tended, as they do today, to occur on take-off or landing, and in neither case would a parachute have been of much use. A plane, it was argued, could glide down to safety. So GQ's plans to market a civil 'chute came to naught.

Hampered by lack of Air Ministry interest, GQ were compelled to tick over by making target plane drogues for their associate, Dagnall. In 1937, following a report from Lieut.-Gen. Sir Andrew Thorne on German paratroop activity, GQ submitted to Mr Leslie Hore-Belisha, War Secretary, a scheme to use parachutes for troops. It was not accepted, but the Air Ministry placed an order for fifty emergency parachutes for Service trials.

The following June, at the opening of Luton airport, a German parachutist intrigued the English crowd with a demonstration of the Eschner parachute, a quick-opening type which used a static line, had no pilot 'chute and shot its canopy out by a spring. The object was to show how easy it was to drop to the ground from an aircraft when as low as 150 feet.

When the Munich crisis plunged an apprehensive Europe into gloom in 1938, the Government woke up. What is your potential? they asked anxiously of GQ; and the company, only too keen for potential, abandoned the old skating rink it had been renting at Woking, girded itself for rearmament and built a new factory. The Government would need all the planes, all the pilots, and hence all the parachutes that it could get.

The factory at Woking was designed to make 24-foot-diameter emergency parachutes, though for some years Quilter and Gregory had been working on a design for a larger version, 28 feet in diameter and with a static line, for paratroops. Now Quilter's uncle returned from a long sojourn in Germany during Hitler's military build-up, during which he had seen a paratroop demonstration which had much impressed him. What, he inquired of his nephew, was Britain doing?

The answer was nothing. When the Russians had not long before made a drop of 1,200 men, 150 machine-guns and 18 light field-guns by parachute and assembled them all in eight minutes, *Flight* magazine reported: 'It is felt in authoritative circles in Britain that although it might prove most useful in general second-class warfare in many parts of the world, it would not be a practical manoeuvre in modern European warfare.'

Many words had been eaten on the parachute question in the previous two decades. Some people were about to begin another meal.

10

THE HEAVENS OPENED

In World War II the parachute's fickle canopy became friend and enemy to both sides in practically every theatre of war. It ushered stricken pilots to safety and airborne armies to victory and defeat, brought food and supplies to the hungry, and flared the way for the bomber's havoc.

The war was a period of intense development for the parachute. As its range of uses widened, so did knowledge about its aerodynamics: it was recognised, for example, that every type of parachute has a critical opening speed—which means that if it is released in the air while an aircraft is travelling above a certain speed, the parachute will 'squid' or remain mostly closed. The critical speed is partly determined by how porous is the canopy fabric: broadly, the less porous it is, the higher the critical opening speed.

Also, experts at last came to appreciate why the parachutes of the pioneers, beginning with Garnerin in 1797, suffered such severe oscillation: because the fabric they used, usually canvas or heavy linen, was *too* impervious to air and caused instability.

Until 1939, silk was in general use for airmen's emergency parachutes. Two advantages of silk are that a large canopy can be fitted into a small pack; it also has a high tensile strength. But silk supplies quickly dried up when war came, and there was a feverish search for alternative materials, not only for emergency 'chutes but to meet the many other needs, which would require new sizes, new porosities, new weaves and new shapes.

During the war, arms and supplies were dropped with high-grade lightweight cotton parachutes, sometimes in clusters for increased stability if they had to bear heavy cargoes. With the discovery of synthetic fibres like nylon, the silk shortage became less crucial. Nylon, which does not deteriorate quickly, was introduced for RAF emergency parachutes and, along with cotton, for dropping paratroops. Jute hessian, a natural fibre, was put into service for sending down mines at sea. The Germans used heavy rayon parachutes for dropping explosives, and, masters of *ersatz* that they were, even developed an ingenious paper parachute of cloth woven from folded paper thread.

No air drops of British fighting men were made before the war, though even as far back as 1918 the commander of the Americans' 1st Brigade in France, Col. William Mitchell, was planning to parachute a whole infantry division behind the enemy lines. Since then, the Russians and Germans had led the way with airborne exercises, and during the Abyssinian war of 1935–6, Italy was reported to have used her Salvator parachute for an air drop of goods including petrol, live animals, medical kits—and even a surgeon. Russia never made large-scale use of paratroops, and even in Finland in late 1939 only comparatively few were dropped— possibly because the Finns were too loyal to produce a willing and useful fifth column.

The parachute's first major military role came in May 1940, when Hitler invaded the Low Countries. Here airborne troops, taking advantage of the flat terrain, were able to establish bridgeheads, create confusion, preoccupy the energies of the Dutch Army, and thrive on the all-too-willing aid of a fruitful supply of Dutch traitors.

On June 22, with France overrun and on the point of surrendering, Winston Churchill wrote to his Chief of Staff: 'We ought to have a corps of at least 5,000 parachute troops . . . I hear something is being done already to form such a corps but only, I believe, on a very small scale. Advantage must be taken of the summer to train these forces, who can none the less play their part meanwhile as shock troops in home defence.'

The response was rapid. A few weeks later, at Ringway, Manchester civil airport, at what came to be called the Central Landing Establishment, Britain began training her new paratroops (and, later, glider troops). She did so by consigning them from the dark wombs of half a dozen cumbersome, cramped, smelly, improvised Whitley bombers. The first jump at Tatton Park was made by the 'pull off' method, soon abandoned, from a platform at the tail-end of the plane, and others through apertures in the floor. All instruction then, as now, was carried out by officers and N.C.O.s of the RAF's Physical Fitness Branch.

All went fairly smoothly for 135 descents, using the standard Irvin 28 feet flat diameter trainer parachute (24 feet for the RAF emergency version). The ripcord was adapted for automatic deployment by static line, one end of which was hooked into a cable inside the aircraft, the other to a breaker cord, thence to the ripcord, on the jumper's pack. But the parachute for the 136th jump, by an R.A.S.C. driver, failed to open and he was killed instantly. The next day, with 200-pound dummies attached, three more failed.

Jumping stopped for five days while a solution was sought. Raymond Quilter, of the GQ Parachute Company, came up with the idea of substituting rigging-lines-first deployment for the traditional canopy-first, so that the parachute would not open until well clear of the plane. Quilter retained the Irvin canopy and harness, but redesigned the packing system. The canopy was stowed in a bag attached by static line to the aircraft, but the rigging lines were packed on a flap over the mouth of the bag. This method, incorporated into the famous 'X' type parachute for paratroopers, and later the 'statichute', was to earn Quilter a Government award of £27,500 after the war.

However, the unpopularity, unsuitability, and danger of the Whitley bomber for training caused pressure to be brought to bear on the Air Ministry to substitute the more suitable Bombay. Appeals were of no avail. 'If you don't like the Whitley,' said the Ministry in effect, 'then don't have paratroops.' The War Office surrendered, and the Whitleys were retained.

With the similarly unpopular Wellington, the Whitley was the training medium until the introduction of Dakotas, with side exits for jumpers, later in the war. Until then the holes in the floor, rather like funnels which narrowed towards the bottom, took an unofficial toll of bloody casualties in plenty, as trainees smashed their faces on the sides when they passed through.

The unhappy Whitley, of which gloom seemed to be an ever-present co-pilot, cast a shadow on morale at a time when encouragement was most needed. In September 1940, 342 officers and men of the newly-formed irregulars called Commandos, which were intended to function as independent units, were recruited for parachute training. No fewer than thirty jibbed at the jump through the floor as the red warning light turned to green; two were killed through parachute failure, and twenty were either found unsuitable or suffered injury.

Soon afterwards, Commando paratroops carried out Britain's first airborne raid, on the Apulia aqueduct in Southern Italy. Through no fault of theirs, it was not a success: a crucial pier turned out to be made of reinforced concrete instead of the anticipated stone, and withstood their quarter-ton of explosives. All that gave way was the Italians' sang-froid at the audacity of it.

More productive by far was the paratroops' next raid, on Bruneval, near Le Havre, where in February 1942 a combined force attacked a radiolocation (radar) station and escaped, to gun-boats waiting offshore, with vital pieces of equipment, data, and several prisoners.

Casualties on the battlefield were expected and inevitable; but in training, theoretically avoidable. In fact, at first injuries and worse were disconcertingly high at Ringway. To win their blue paratrooper's wings, recruits had to make a controlled jump from a tower, two jumps from a captive balloon (much disliked because of the impression it gave of height), and five more from aircraft. But of 543 men who underwent the two weeks' course at Ringway towards the end of 1941, 38 received serious injury, including fractured spines and broken legs. Three months later, 48 out of 238 on a similar course were injured and two men killed.

Investigations established a mysterious tendency for parachute rigging lines to twist, thus delaying the canopy's opening. Each parachute was equipped with four lift-webs—strips of webbing extending upwards for about three feet to where the rigging lines sprang from rings up to the canopy—and these gave a measure of control and steerability when pulled. When the lines twisted, this was impossible and the 'chute drifted helplessly.

With each serious injury, suggestions of providing a reserve parachute, a part of the equipment of even a fully trained paratrooper today, were renewed but rejected on the grounds of cost and weight: the main 'chute already weighed 25 pounds, it was argued. Group Captain Maurice Newnham, the C.O., himself offered a solution. He devised a new method of packing the rigging lines so that their loops sat vertically, and with each loop enclosed in its own canvas pocket to eliminate risk of entanglement.

Leslie Irvin, who made the prototype at Letchworth, was strongly in favour of this modification; so was Air Marshal Trafford Leigh-Mallory, C.-in-C. Fighter Command, who convened a conference to discuss parachuting equipment. The discussion came to an end, however, when a member of an Air Ministry directorate, fresh from operational duties at his office in Whitehall, brandished his elegant cigarette holder and announced that his department was quite satisfied with progress already being made. So nothing more was heard of Newnham's idea, and equipment remained as it was.

Among the thousands who were trained as parachutists were agents to be dropped by Special Operations Executive into occupied Europe. More than 1,300 members of the gallant French section passed through Ringway. None of them was injured during training, but six were killed during their drops into France. In one case the plane went in too low; one man landed badly; two were killed through faulty parachutes; one because he forgot to hook up his static line; another was killed for reasons that died with him.

Some equipment was taken down by the agents. The lift-webs on their harnesses were made specially long, so that radios and other items could be hung there during the descent. A continual flow of supplies was maintained to agents in the field; in total about 120,000 shock-resisting packages and containers found their way by parachute into France. Packers became so expert that even 200 bottles of printing ink, destined for an underground news-paper, arrived without a single casualty.

Immense care was of course taken in packing man-carrying parachutes, too. Each one took about 25 minutes to fold, stow and be inspected. To avoid the depredations of damp and creasing, packers had to remove an unused parachute from its pack after two months. And it could not be used for more than twenty-five descents.

Packing was the preserve of members of the then Women's Auxiliary Air Force (now the Women's Royal Air Force). Packer and repairer were recognised trades for women aged between seventeen and forty-three, and there were about 2,800 of them throughout the country. One of the routine tasks was tracking the career of each parachute in a record book so that it was not overworked and did not escape repair.

At Ringway, the odds against a fatal jump in 1942 were about 6,000 to 1, which was cut in less than three years to one in 100,000. Accidents were due to bad jumping or faulty equipment rather than careless packing. Signs above the packers' heads were a constant reminder of their responsibility: 'A man's life depends on every parachute you pack'—and despite the tedious succession of jokes from parachutists about being able to draw a second 'chute if the first did not work, they treated their task with dedicated seriousness.

For thirty-two years, confessed one padre after his first jump from a training balloon, his whole trust had been reposed in God; but for a few seconds, until his parachute opened, his confidence was transferred to a WAAF parachute packer. Not without good cause: by 1945, half a million descents had been made by 60,000 paratroops passing through the No. 1 Parachute Training School, but only one fatal accident could ever be traced to faulty packing.

The girls brought a certain feminine sensitivity to their work which helped to sustain, in more than one sense, the men who donned the parachutes. One of the Ringway packers, G. D. Martineau, crystallised her feelings with a moving little poem, the first and last verses of which ran:

> When they posted me here to the section,
> I was free as the pitiless air,
> Unashamed of confessed imperfection,
> Having no sort of burden to bear;
> I was not an incurable slacker;
> Neat, not fussy—I fancied of old;
> But today I'm a parachute packer,
> And my heart takes a turn with each fold. . .
>
> So is conscience awakened and care born
> In the heart of a negligent maid.
> Fickle Aeolus, fight for the Airborne,
> Whom I strive with frail fingers to aid.
> Give my heroes kind wind and fair weather,
> Let no parachute sidle or slump.
> For today we go warring together,
> And my soul will be there at the jump.[1]

In many lands did the men of the Parachute Regiment, and the thoughts of those in England, take wing and go 'warring together'. Given their sobriquet, the 'Red Devils', by reluctant German admirers in North Africa in 1942, they fought with immense panache and distinction, sometimes against hopeless odds, on many fronts and often on no cohesive front at all. In terms of numbers, none of their actions compared with the scale of the German invasion of Crete in 1941, the first occasion in history on which an island was captured from the air.

It was just as well. Though Crete fell in eleven days, the price of this victory was too high even for Hitler. Of the 25,000 German troops landed by parachute and glider and from the sea, well over 4,000 were killed and 2,000 wounded; and 170 out of 600 transport aircraft were destroyed. Never again did he try

[1] *The Red Beret* by H. St George Saunders (Michael Joseph, 1950).

another airborne attack on this scale, and plans to invade Malta using paratroops were abandoned.

British paratroops fought in North Africa, Italy, Sicily, during the invasion of France, and the Rhine crossing. At Arnhem, 10,000 paratroops earned their own brand of glory behind the enemy lines, three-quarters of them killed, wounded or missing. From the days when they first consigned their lives to the fragment of fabric which cracked open on the air above them, the paratroops were accustomed to living near to death. Red Devils they may have been, but to the peoples of the sad lands of occupied Europe, as they watched the paratroops descend from the heavens, like floating mushrooms, they were angels indeed.

Many non-combatant soldiers among the British, objecting to participating in aggressive war on principle, nevertheless had a tougher war than most with the Royal Army Medical Corps or Non-Combatant Corps, having been attached to paratroop units with the Parachute Field Ambulance.

They were usually equipped with revolvers, but only for self-defence and the protection of the wounded, though some refused to carry guns at all and landed on D-Day completely unarmed.

The Parachute Field Ambulance dropped on to the battlefield with the main attacking force, bringing down with them canisters of medical supplies. Immediately they landed they set up field surgical and dressing stations. Surgeons who officered these units often carried out serious operations with the enemy only a few yards away.

The axiomatic toughness of paratroops concealed a compassion for the wounded, whichever side they were on. One British staff sergeant in the Parachute Field Ambulance, a non-combatant volunteer, was cycling with a message to headquarters during the Sicily invasion when he spotted a German soldier, seriously wounded, and obviously near death, lying in a doorway. He stopped, crossed the road and gave the German a shot of morphine, returned to his bicycle and was himself immediately hit by an enemy mortar shell. Despite this, he went on to rescue some of his wounded compatriots under fire, for which he was awarded the Military Medal.

R. M. Wingfield, in *The Only Way Out*,[1] also pays tribute to the German paratroops, for whom, he says, 'we felt quite a professional affection'. They fought cleanly, he says, and treated prisoners with the respect they expected from the British. He recalls an incident in which two German stretcher-bearers, seeing one of a couple of British stretcher-bearers injured by a mortar-bomb while dealing with a casualty, went out themselves into no-man's-land and carried the injured British, under the direction of their compatriot, to the British lines.

'Waving farewell, they doubled back to the wood. We cheered them all the way back. A 12-hour truce followed. No-one had the heart to spoil this gesture by firing. So, temporarily, the war stopped. Next morning they were gone.'

Unlike the Allies, Hitler, though originally in the van of para-troop warfare, never fully appreciated their strategic value. Consequently, the German paratroops, the Fallschirmjäger, formed in the mid-1930s from volunteers, and regarded as the flower of German manhood, were rarely used as airborne troops after the costly Crete operation of 1941. Instead they filled the more mundane role of élite infantrymen. On their formation, they numbered about a thousand: by the end of the war there were 250,000.

The first parachute they used, the R.Z.1, was not entirely satis-factory in that it gave the jumper a severe shock when it opened. To lessen this, paratroops took to making spread-eagled dives when they left the plane. Nor did the R.Z.1 always fully open, and too many landings were made too fast. In 1940 this parachute gave way to the R.Z.16 which, though a sound parachute, lacked the quick release device provided on later models.

Like the British man-carrying parachute, the German version, made of silk, artificial silk or Perlon, was camouflaged because it too would otherwise have presented an easy target on the ground. When the Germans introduced camouflage, however, their

[1] Hutchinson, 1955.

paratroops protested because they thought the dyes made the canopies less likely to deploy and slowed it down when it did. This notion was quite baseless, but they were not satisfied until the High Command ordered that all camouflaged parachutes should be dusted with French chalk before packing!

★

The creation in World War II of huge and powerful airborne armies, with warfare more mobile than ever before, called the parachute into use on a spectacular scale. In some theatres of war, like Burma, it was often the only means of getting supplies to armies thrust deep into enemy territory where landing aircraft was impossible.

'The vulnerable artery is the line of communication winding through the jungle,' said Chindit leader Major-General Orde Wingate. 'Have no line of communication on the jungle floor. Bring in the goods, like Father Christmas, down the chimney.' And bring in the goods they did. Under the parachute's fluttering canopy, millions of tons went 'down the chimney' to Allied troops, the Chindits among them.

In 1943 a vast number of parachutes for air supply was needed, not simply for the Chindits but also for the main body of the 14th Army, poised to attack. Then came bad news for the 14th Army's commander, Lieut.-Gen. (later Field Marshal) Slim. Parachute supplies from India would be far below their needs, and because there was a parachute shortage throughout the world, none would be forthcoming from Britain either.

Slim faced two possibilities; either reducing the scale of his plans or seeking an alternative to parachute silk. First he thought of using paper, like the Germans, but the paper being manufactured in Calcutta was unfortunately the wrong sort. So he settled for jute, and with the cooperation of Calcutta businessmen, who showed a remarkable lack of interest in payment, the 'parajute' was a reality within a month. It had no large vent in the apex, but several smaller ones all over, and it was only about one-seventh less efficient than the standard silk parachute.

The parajutes were not intended for man-carrying, but about 100,000 of them were used for supply-dropping in the Burma campaign at a cost of about £1 each compared with £20 for the standard product. Slim's reward for using his imagination in time of dire need was admonishment from higher authority for failing to order parachutes through the proper channels!

When the war began, in 1939, there was little call for supplies to be dropped from the air. Britain's biggest container was made to take only 150 pounds of supplies, and its parent parachute was only 14 feet in flat diameter. But as our airborne army built up, so did the means of delivery. On D-Day, the RAF were dropping jeeps and anti-tank guns weighing 1½ tons each, borne on clusters of three or four parachutes 60 feet in diameter to maintain stability.

The large parachutes were not completely satisfactory because they were difficult to maintain in the field. Almost as war ended, a 42-foot parachute, with shaped gores instead of straight-sided ones, was replacing the 60-foot version. Clusters of these could be released safely at aircraft speeds of up to 200 m.p.h.

Originally, heavy loads were dropped using the static line system employed by paratroops. It was first tried when dropping an airborne lifeboat on a triple cluster of 32-foot parachutes, but because this caused damage to the aircraft a new method of release was developed. First, a small auxiliary parachute (like an ordinary parachute but with several vanes running up the centre) would emerge, and this would pull out a 12-foot retarder parachute, which had two different fabric porosities in the canopy and was designed to open suddenly. Below the retarder were the main parachute packs, from which the canopies would be hauled out by the weight of the fast-falling lifeboat.

Containers to accompany paratroops were dropped from the bomb bays of aircraft. Ideally, they had to go down in the middle of a 'stick' of men, so as to be quickly on hand at ground level. To prevent it fouling paratroopers' parachutes, a delay mechanism was introduced: a spring-loaded metal arm which could be adjusted to allow opening after one-half to six seconds. The container, with its parachute coloured for easy identification, would then fall below the stick of parachutists and open without endangering them.

The Germans, not satisfied with containers merely for supplies, dreamed up an advanced version for men—a 'human bomb'. Four parachutes supported the container, which was nine feet long and six in diameter, with three saboteurs inside complete with weapons. On reaching ground, the men would carry out their task, return and lock themselves inside the container and lie waiting for a low-flying aircraft to sweep in and hook them aloft without landing.

The parachute was the vehicle of the first of Hitler's 'secret weapons', the non-contact magnetic or acoustic sea-mine, which began to take its toll of Allied shipping only a few days after the war began. German planes dropped these parachute mines in the Thames and Humber estuaries, and Harwich harbour, on November 21, 1939. The following night, more were dropped at Shoeburyness and one was captured intact and dismantled to disclose 660 pounds of explosives.

The British also dropped their magnetic mines by parachute— the jute hessian type. The mines were cylindrical and blunt-ended rather than streamlined, because they did not need to fall at speed. The whole point of the parachute, in fact, was to ensure a soft landing so that the mine's sensitive delayed action mechanism was undamaged.

'Land mines', which were in fact naval parachute mines that exploded on contact after descending in deadly silence, were for a time a most devastating agent of destruction in air raids on London. The parachute's drag and slow descent ensured that the explosion was on the surface of the ground, thus creating the maximum area of damage. No one who has seen the results of the parachute mine is likely to forget it.

Many of these mines failed to explode, thus dislocating A.R.P. and other services which had never expected to deal with them anyway. On one occasion an unexploded mine stopped fireboats from getting to blitz-torn London above Tower Bridge. Another unexploded mine, dropped in April 1941, put the entire east end of St Paul's Cathedral in jeopardy, until a Royal Naval disposal squad had dealt with it.

Meanwhile, the parachute was employed in the recovery, out over the Baltic, of practice A-5 rockets (the German precursors of the V.2, of which 1,115 were to rain down on a helpless London later in the war), another of Hitler's secret weapons.

Reconnaissance flares were dropped over German territory on cotton parachutes. Although used throughout the war, they did not always open satisfactorily, and often failed to linger long enough to be of value and fell too quickly. They were designed before the war, and thus before high-speed aircraft were put into service and before the importance of canopy fabrics was fully appreciated. Because it was too late to amend the design, the war ended with a product that was less than ideal.

For anti-submarine attacks, the British used a slow-falling parachute flare which dropped at about six feet per second, or about a third of the speed of a paratrooper's descent. Para*sheets*, which acted like parachutes but were formed of strips of fabric rather than gores, were used for these. To economise on silk, they were of a man-made fibre called Celanese Fortisan, which took up little space when folded. A pair of parasheets were used for each flare to increase stability.

Airfields and ports in England were defended with the aid of a cleverly contrived device called 'P.A.C.', the parachute-and-cable rocket. Marauding German planes, zooming in for low-level attacks, suddenly found steel cables snaking up 500 feet into the sky ahead of them, with a parachute at the end to keep the cable long enough in the air to ward off danger.

The P.A.C. was adapted by the Royal Navy's Directorate of Miscellaneous Weapon Development for use at sea and designed by a company which normally made rockets for life-saving. After much experimentation with linen and nylon cord supplied by a West End store, the team produced a strong canopy and rigging lines. Soon, merchant ships were equipped with P.A.C., and in 1941 reports filtered in giving evidence of its value. The small convoy vessel *Fireglow*, for example, was caught in a big air attack when the mate, standing by one of its two P.A.C.s, suddenly yanked the firing lanyard and up shot the cable, neatly slicing the wing off a German bomber. Soon enemy pilots were taking home worried stories about the mysterious and lethal 'spirals' which keep appearing from nowhere.

When the P.A.C. left the secret list in 1943, it was known to have brought down nine German aircraft and saved at least thirty-five Allied ships from bombing attacks.

11

BY A SILKEN THREAD

BRITAIN'S BOMBING offensive in the first two years of the war was disappointingly wasteful and woefully inaccurate. By the end of 1941 only three per cent of the weight of all bombs dropped on Germany were finding their way to within five miles of their targets. In the second half of the war, thanks to the Halifaxes, Lancasters and Mosquitoes of the RAF's Pathfinder Force, formed in 1942 and equipped with new navigational aids, raids on Germany became devastatingly successful. To this success the parachute made no small contribution.

The Pathfinders were an élite corps assembled and commanded throughout their three years' life by a brilliant navigator and former Imperial Airways pilot, Group Captain (later Air Vice-Marshal) Donald Bennett. Their purpose was to lead and light the way for our bombers over enemy territory and signpost their dropping points.

There was much opposition to the Force initially, not least from Bomber Command C.-in-C. Air Marshal Arthur Harris, who disliked the prospect of having to cream off some of his best air crews to form it. But today, insists Bennett with the advantage of hindsight, the Pathfinder concept was 'the greatest single factor in victory', making way as it did for repeated stabs at Germany's industrial heart.

When the war began, magnesium parachute flares were found to be unreliable. They were not accurate, principally because the time fusing was rarely properly adjusted; nor did aircraft ever seem to be at the planned height. And the back-glare from the flares was so strong as to blind air crews and offset any advantage from illumination of the ground.

When the Pathfinders were formed, Bennett counteracted the glare by installing an umbrella-like hood between the flare and the

(*Above*) Skydivers 'swim' towards each other to form a star in space. (*Right*) Tracy Rixon, with her multiple aerofoil Papillon, a French parachute, touches down during the 1972 British National Parachute Championships in which she won the women's title.

An Avro Vulcan jet plane (*above*) is braked to a
stop with an RFD-GQ parachute. In America
(*below left*) 'smoke jumpers' descend by parachute
to fight forest fires. (*Below right*) from da Vinci to
Apollo—Number 15 splashes down in the Pacific
under its parachutes, one of which failed to open.

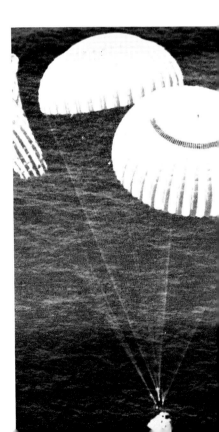

main canopy of the parachute. Because the height of release had to be flexible, and match varying conditions, he abandoned the time-governed release fuse and substituted a barometric device so that the parachute opened at a pre-selected height.

The flare was used to light up targets on the ground, and it was followed down by the target indicator, or T.I., a collection of Roman candles which exploded two or three hundred feet above the ground and continued its display after it had landed.

The parachute flare was especially valuable in sky-marking, when cloud was too dense for bomb-aimers to see target indicators on the ground, though many of Bennett's colleagues scoffed at his idea until they saw the results. Dropped above the cloud according to readings from the Pathfinders' radar devices, H2S or 'Oboe', the flare would burn in varying colours, depending on the code chosen for the day or the particular operation. It burned for four minutes and was dropped in such a position that it would be accurately placed after three minutes of drift. Bomb aimers would drop their bombs the moment the flare entered their sights —in theory, exactly on target.

This tactic, employed throughout the latter part of the war, figured in the highly successful attack on Essen on January 9, 1943, which was made through thick cloud. It was obvious to the Germans that blind bombing was being used, but Hitler could hardly bring himself to believe it. So angered was he, according to Pathfinder-leader Air Vice-Marshal Bennett, that he threatened some of his intelligence advisers with execution.

The parachute flare was in brave hands indeed. Between the time the Pathfinders were formed and the end of the war they flew more than 50,000 individual sorties against 3,440 targets. Their planes were often unarmed, and they were required to make a tour of sixty operational sorties against the bomber crew's normal thirty. It is hardly surprising that 3,600 Pathfinders were killed in action, about one in ten of Bomber Command's entire wartime toll.

For Air Vice-Marshal Bennett, the parachute proved doubly valuable: not only did it contribute to the achievements of his

Pathfinder Force, it also saved his life. Bennett was commanding a squadron of Halifaxes, which was given the task of bombing the German warship Tirpitz, near Trondheim in Norway. The object was to drop five 1,000-pound spherical mines down the banks of the fjord and explode them against the ship's hull under water.

Bennett's aircraft came in for the bombing run at only 200 feet, but was badly hit by anti-aircraft fire. The crew kept it on course, but when they arrived over where they thought the ship was, they cursed their luck: it was hidden beneath an artificial camouflage 'fog'. The Halifax, a starboard engine blazing fiercely, turned to make another run. It released the mines as accurately as it was able, then tackled the next obstacle, one which was literally almost insuperable. For ahead of them soared a 3,000-foot-high mountain range, and both their starboard engines were now burning. Bennett, realising the plane was certain to crash, throttled the outer port engine in an effort to stabilise, and gave the order to abandon aircraft.

At this point, to his horror, Bennett became suddenly aware that he alone was without a parachute. It was stowed away down the fuselage. Fortunately, Colgan, his flight engineer, found it for him and clipped it on to the quick connector snap-hooks on his chest. (This was the usual method of parachute attachment for bomber crews, who needed their hands free and had to be able to move about the plane unencumbered: fighter pilots wore seat-packs which they sat on like cushions in their cockpits.)

The Halifax was losing height so rapidly that there was hardly time to jump. Bennett leapt through the hatch, pulled the ripcord and the parachute opened a few moments before he hit the snow. He and his colleagues managed to dodge the Germans and, after many adventures, escaped home via Sweden.

Thus, another member was recruited to the Caterpillar Club, Irvin's exclusive association of airmen who had survived an emergency jump using an Irvin-designed parachute. Since the club's inauguration in 1922, there have been thousands of 'caterpillars'—33,000 in the European branch alone, most of them qualifying for membership during the Second World War.

Irvin himself, however, never qualified as a 'caterpillar' because although during his life-time he made more than 300 parachute descents, he never had to make a jump during an emergency.

The advent of the war and the tremendous demand for para-chutes brought great prosperity to Irvin and his Letchworth factory, where he remained practically throughout the war even though he was an American citizen. In fact, he developed a fierce patriotism on Britain's behalf: he would travel round Letchworth on a bicycle, apparently to save petrol, and he would give frequent pep-talks to his factory employees over the loud-speaker system, urging that every minute possible be devoted to the war effort and parachute production in particular. Yet he also enjoyed long talks with them, and would throw a party or give a cowboy film show on the flimsiest pretext.

One day, hearing that several American airmen had baled out in the vicinity of the town, Irvin sent a car post-haste to collect them. Within the hour, while still trembling from the shock of the jump, the airmen found themselves faced with another ordeal —that of making a morale-boosting appearance on stage in the factory and saying a few encouraging words to the workers.

A circus performer to the end, Irvin enjoyed the chance to remind others of his show business origins. In *Prelude to Glory*[1] Group Captain Maurice Newnham recalls how Irvin would enter-tain at Ringway with his favourite parlour trick: standing on his head against a piano, playing 'I Want to be Happy' and drinking a glass of beer, all at the same time.

★

One Caterpillar's escape record eclipsed even Lindbergh's in the 1920s (see Chapter 8): it belonged to the young RAF fighter pilot, Tony Woods-Scawen, who managed to avoid disaster eleven times: he made four forced landings, three crash landings

[1] Sampson Low, Marston, 1947.

and four parachute jumps. His first escape, which gained him membership of the Caterpillar Club, was in June 1940 when his Hurricane was shot down over Dieppe. After being presumed missing, he turned up eight days later at Tangmere carrying the parachute that had saved him. He had slipped through from behind the German lines and joined a B.E.F. unit evacuating from France. He successfully made parachute escapes three times more, but his fifth jump was made when his plane was too low, and he hit the ground before his parachute had time to develop.

The little gold Caterpillar brooch is usually the indication of a host of fascinating adventures experienced by the wearer, sometimes poignant, sometimes hair-raising, and often commanding admiration.

In the troubled 'thirties, Ernst Udet, the German ace who parachuted down after a dog-fight in World War I, had become an Irvin 'caterpillar'. In July 1934 the tail of his Curtiss Hawk broke off during dive-bombing practice over Templehof airport, Berlin. His parachute opened just in time, with only feet to spare. Now, during World War II, as a high-ranking Luftwaffe officer under Goering, Udet was helping to make 'caterpillars' of British pilots.

One of the unluckiest of these was undoubtedly Flight-Lieut. James Nicolson, a Hurricane pilot of 249 Squadron who, on a cloudless afternoon in August 1940, won Fighter Command's only V.C. of the war.

Nicolson had never been able to get a shot at a German before, so when a group of Junkers 88s droned into the Gosport area he thought he held out a strong chance of making his first 'kill'. As he and his flight flew in, however, Nicolson was dismayed to see a squadron of Spitfires move in and shoot down all the Junkers before Nicolson's Hurricanes could get within range.

Turning back, disappointed, Nicolson suddenly found himself being attacked. Cannon shells ripped through his plane. His left eye was injured by splinters, his right trouser leg was partly torn off, and his left foot was hit. Flames leapt up in the cockpit.

Just as he was preparing to bale out, Nicolson spotted his

attacker shoot past him. He sat back again and decided to take his revenge. Ignoring his own plight, he dived down after the Messerschmitt, firing rounds by the score until it crashed. By this time, Nicolson was in an appalling condition, his hands horribly burnt, his instrument panel smashed and melting from the heat. Desperately, he heaved himself away from the remains of his charred seat belt and threw himself out.

Luckily, his parachute was undamaged and it opened as if nothing had happened. Nicolson sailed earthwards, bleeding from his wounds, only to be shot in the legs by an over-zealous British civil defence worker. He survived his ordeal and flew again to win the D.F.C., but was killed in an air crash in the Far East at the end of the war.

Twice the parachute came to the aid of Group Captain Douglas Bader. Bader lost both legs in a flying accident in 1931, was invalided out of the RAF and fought a determined and ultimately successful campaign with the authorities to re-join. He rose to the acting rank of Wing Commander and was a front-line pilot who fought with great distinction in the Battle of Britain. According to Paul Brickhill, his biographer, Bader was the best fighter leader and tactician of World War II and figured among the best pilots.

Bader qualified for membership of the Caterpillar Club on August 9, 1941 on a fighter sweep over northern France, two months after the strangest parachutist of the war, Hitler's deputy, Rudolf Hess, dropped from his plane in Scotland on his alleged peace-making mission.

Shortly after Bader's Spitfire had crossed the coast, a Messerschmitt 109 intercepted at 24,000 feet and attacked. In the ensuing dog-fight, Bader suddenly saw chunks flying off his plane, and as he glanced round saw that the tail unit had practically disappeared.

As its nose went down, the Spitfire went into a vertical dive and started to spin. He knew there was only one way out now—baling out, if he could. He heaved himself up with his hands, got his artificial left leg outside, and hauled on the other. Nothing happened—it was firmly lodged in the cockpit. Then suddenly, after long seconds, the leather straps snapped and Bader shot out of the plane, but leaving his right leg still jammed in the cockpit.

The Spitfire had dropped through the sky for 20,000 feet over Bethune before Bader baled out by parachute. He made a painful landing on his remaining artificial leg, which pulled up into his chest.

He was captured by the Germans and taken to St Omer hospital. When the doctors saw what was left of his legs, they had no need to ask his name, for to the Germans Bader's name was almost as legendary as it was among his own countrymen.

Bader asked for the missing leg to be reclaimed from the wrecked Spitfire, and the Germans not only reclaimed it but did a brilliant job of repairing it. Meanwhile, with Goering's permission, they also radioed the British to send a spare. The Germans asked for the leg to be landed by Lysander, which would be guaranteed free passage. There would have been a British fighter escort to the French coast, then Messerschmitts would take over. But the British were having none of this. Dismissing the German offer as a propaganda ploy, they planned to drop the leg by parachute from a Blenheim sent over on a normal bombing raid.

Bader was no model prisoner of the Germans: he saw it as his duty to be as difficult and obstructive as possible. It was shortly after his recapture following the first of his attempted escapes that his RAF friends at Tangmere kept their appointment. As the British planes streaked home from a bombing raid, they flew over St Omer airfield, leaving a long yellow box to float down by parachute. It was addressed to the commandant and contained Bader's spare right leg.

At the end of the European war, Bader, now with a double D.S.O., a double D.F.C. and the acting rank of Wing Commander, led his fighter pilots in triumph once more across the southern skies, at the head of the first Battle of Britain fly-past on September 15, 1945.

The most incredible exploit involving any escaping airman was the jump of a Lancaster rear-gunner, Flight Sergeant Nicholas Alkemade. He miraculously survived a desperate leap from his crippled plane at 18,000 feet over Germany—without a parachute at all.

It happened on the night of March 24, 1944, when Alkemade, veteran of a dozen night raids over Berlin, climbed into his lonely gun turret and joined yet another 300-bomber raid on the German capital. The outward flight was uneventful, and after dropping its 4,000-pound blockbuster and a host of incendiaries in what seemed a remarkably trouble-free trip, the plane turned for home.

Then without warning a roaming Junkers 88 attacked. The Lancaster's turret shattered as the German plane blasted its tail. Alkemade replied with his Brownings, and after long bursts saw the Junkers plunge earthwards, fatally crippled. His satisfaction was shortlived, however, for the Lancaster itself was now a mass of flames, which poured down the fuselage towards Alkemade's turret. He made for his parachute stowage, but the fire got there first. His last hope vanished.

Alkemade now faced exactly the terrifying dilemma of parachute-less pilots of World War I: to perish with the plane or jump, with certain death a sound each-way bet. Alkemade jumped.

By all natural laws, Alkemade should have died, his body smashed like Robert Cocking's a century earlier. But he didn't. Ninety incredible seconds later, stunned, bleeding, burned, but alive, Alkemade crashed through the branches of a pine forest and hit a bank of snow. When the Germans found him, they did not believe him. It must be a trick. How could a man fall three and a half miles and live? Only when they realised that webbing straps on part of his harness were still folded and tied down, and when they retrieved his ripcord and cable from the wrecked Lancaster twenty miles away, did they accept his story.

Alkemade did not expect the feting staged by the Germans; he was content just to be alive. But for posterity, they drew up a hand-written certificate to corroborate his story, which was signed by a British flight-lieutenant and two flight-sergeants in the prison camp.

Thus did Alkemade prove what till then was an untenable proposition: that to make a safe bale-out, a parachute is not strictly necessary. But it helps.

★

The two major dangers for escaping airmen were, firstly, being shot at as they floated down on parachutes—a practice forbidden under a draft code drawn up by the Commission of Jurists at the Hague in 1923. The code had not been adopted by Britain, but the rule concerned was generally observed by her, if not by Germany. In 1941, Sir Samuel Hoare, Air Secretary, revealed that attacks had been made by the Germans on twelve British pilots, four of whom had been killed.

Yet just before the fall of France in 1940, the Germans had complained that their pilots were being fired upon by the French, who were at that time no doubt on the *qui vive* for enemy paratroops, and shot at them by accident. Goering threatened to kill fifty French prisoners for every German pilot shot in this way.

The Italians showed particular viciousness towards Allied pilots in North Africa, and one Italian newspaper even urged in 1943 that a good way for Italian anti-aircraft gunners to practise would be to aim at Allied pilots as they came down on their parachutes.

A clear distinction was and is made of course between paratroops and escaping airmen. The Manual of Military Law states that 'it is lawful to fire on airborne troops and others engaged, or who appear to be engaged, on hostile missions whilst such persons are descending from aircraft, in particular over territory in control of the opposing forces, whether or not that aircraft has been disabled. It is, on the other hand, unlawful to fire at other persons descending by parachute from disabled aircraft.'

The other risk, admittedly on a smaller scale, was of attack once a baled-out airman had been taken prisoner. Under a decree issued by Hitler in 1942, some Allied Commandos and paratroops were executed in captivity—in contravention of the rules of war protecting prisoners. When the bombing of Germany was stepped up in 1943, civilians were actively encouraged to lynch airmen who escaped by parachute.

It was alleged during the Nuremberg trials in 1946 by Schellenberg, deputy to German security chief Ernst Kaltenbrunner, that he heard Kaltenbrunner say: 'All officers of the S.D. and Security Police are to be informed that pogroms of the populace against English and American terror-fliers are not to be interfered with. On the contrary, this hostile mood is to be encouraged.'

12

GOING WITH A BANG

AIR, WHICH helped to provide the raw material of lift when man took wing and the drag of a parachute when his new toy failed to work, reacted vengefully when flying came to place a greater dependence on thrust, through the medium of jet-propelled aircraft. Escape by parachute now ceased to be a matter of practical certainty and became more a question of luck.

To the potentially dangerous fact of being off the ground at all were added the twin enemies of intense air pressure and a force many times that of gravity, or 'g', which all too often pressed pilots back into their cockpits and prevented them from baling out. Many would try to undo their safety harness, jettison the cockpit hood and if possible turn the plane upside down and be thrown out by a kind of negative 'g'.

The problem of survival, which for a time soured early jet flight, was emphasised in January 1944 when Squadron Leader Douglas Davie, a test pilot of the Royal Aircraft Establishment, was killed at Farnborough. He was trying to escape from one of the newly introduced Gloster Meteors (later used for the first time to shoot down the German V.1 flying bomb) when one of the engines exploded. Although he managed to get out of the cockpit in the usual way, over the side, he injured himself, lost consciousness in the immense blast of air, and failed to open his parachute. A few months later another pilot was killed testing a Meteor prototype at Glosters.

Some kind of mechanical ejection was clearly urgent, though what the human body could tolerate in terms of violent acceleration was not known, and was now to be studied by the RAF's Institute of Aviation Medicine. Whatever the ultimate solution, the parachute would still fill its traditional role, for the Air Staff had stipulated that mechanical ejection must 'utilise existing safety equipment'. Ejection seats came to be shaped round the parachute back pack, which fitted into a recess behind the airman.

Experiments on a test rig at Farnborough, using a 2,000-foot-long rocket track, showed that a man could stand acceleration of up to twelve times the force of gravity, but not for longer than a tenth of a second. The R.A.E. concluded that to meet all requirements, including being thrown clear of the plane's tail, an ejection seat would have to thrust the crew out at around forty feet per second.

Meantime, at Higher Denham, Buckinghamshire, the problem of escape from high-speed aircraft had engaged the interest of James (now Sir James) Martin, an aeroplane designer and engineer who had four prototype light aircraft to his credit. Martin, an Ulsterman and the son of a farmer, was deeply interested in the power of explosives. One of his wartime inventions was a cockpit hood that could be jettisoned for Spitfires; another was an anti-barrage balloon cable-cutter, an explosive-motivated chisel mounted in the leading edges of the wings of bombers which was used to good effect against the Germans, for example, on raids over the well-defended Dortmund Emms Canal. Martin was now to put explosives to work to save lives—by turning men into 'human cannonballs' on parachutes.

His friend and partner, Captain Valentine Baker, crashed and was killed while testing a prototype aircraft in 1942, so Martin was closely concerned with air hazards—though he admits that no ejection seat could have saved his friend. But it could save others. Early in 1944, an RAF staff officer spoke to Martin of the Meteor pilots' anxiety over the difficulty of escape. The Mark I version was not the main source of concern. This jet, at 445 m.p.h. maximum only a shade faster than existing piston-engined planes, was soon to be followed by 600 m.p.h. models which would make the escape problem acute.

Martin assumed that any device he produced would also have to be fitted to Spitfires and Hurricanes forming the RAF's main fighter force. But in these planes, cockpit space was cramped, and the only workable method seemed to be a swinging arm along the fuselage, fixed forward of the tail fin. The cockpit hood would be jettisoned and the spring-loaded arm, like a highspeed crane, would hoist the pilot up by his parachute harness and fling him clear. He would then pull his ripcord and land safely by parachute.

Sir Stafford Cripps, Minister of Aircraft Production, was impressed with the device, but it was decided—presumably because the day of the Spitfire and Hurricane was almost over—not to put it into production. Instead, Martin concentrated on a system of ejecting pilot and seat together by means of a gun. After making a model of an ejector, which the Air Ministry approved in principle, Martin was given a reconditioned Boulton Paul Defiant, an early World War II fighter, and experiments with the 'bang seat' began.

The British, it appears, were not the first in the ejection seat field. There is evidence that the Germans were carrying out work along these lines a good deal earlier, though Sir James Martin, like Irvin with his ripcord parachute, quickly strode ahead and set up a commanding lead in technical development and adaptation which has never been overtaken. Today he is acknowledged the world over as the father of the ejection seat.

The Germans had begun to experiment even in 1938. They fitted a Junkers 88 with a compressed air powered seat the following year. Eventually they were installed on the Messerschmitt 262, Heinkel 219A-7 and 262A, and Dornier 335A-6. But although by the end of the war about sixty Luftwaffe pilots and crew had made emergency ejections in action, the German device was not an unmixed blessing. The thrust of the compressed air gun was so powerful that spinal injuries became disturbingly frequent, and a thorough investigation into the limits of pilots' endurance and tolerance of impact was in progress even as they surrendered in 1945.

In the autumn of 1944, James Martin made a test rig at Denham —a 16-foot-high tripod, one of its legs resembling a children's playground slide, up which the ejection seat would be fired at high speed. A ratchet stop was provided to measure effects on the human body of increasingly severe accelerations.

Medical experts were pessimistic, but not the guinea-pig who cheerfully offered himself to make the first live test ride, an Irish experimental fitter, 27-year-old Bernard Lynch. He first rode the rig on January 24, 1945, starting with shots to 4 feet 8 inches and ending, after more powerful cartridges had been fitted into the seat, at 10 feet (unpleasantly, by all accounts). Tests using dummies as well as human beings were made, and detailed measurements of 'g' loads and the amount of explosive required. One visiting reporter was given something unexpected to write about when he volunteered for a live test and came down with a crushed vertebra. Some of the instruments failed to withstand the test shocks too.

Martin then turned his attention to the human spine. He studied a skeleton and watched hospital operations in order to learn more about the spine's construction. As a result he re-arranged the firing of the seat and, by introducing a second cartridge fired automatically by the first, achieved a smoother acceleration. He also re-designed the seat's footrests so that the spine's vertebrae would sit trim and square to each other, and introduced a face screen method of exploding the cartridges.

The face-screen, or blind, was made of canvas and attached to the firing handle above the pilot's head; when pulled down it would cover his face. This fulfilled a double role: it kept him sitting upright and protected his face from the deadly rush of air after the seat had been shot out of the aircraft.

These improvements paid off. In no time, Lynch was able to experience a 'very soft' ride of 26 feet 3 inches up a new 65-foot test rig, with no unpleasant side-effects at all.

Three days after VE-Day, on May 11, 1945, James Martin achieved his first ejection from a moving aircraft. The seat was loaded with bags of shot to represent the pilot, and these were caught in a net to conserve the equipment. The next day, at Wittering airfield, he used a dummy, and in the following weeks six more dummy ejections were made at Beaulieu from the Defiant at speeds ranging up to 300 m.p.h.

Martin was much encouraged by his successes using artificial 'cargo'. But although he could calculate the degree of force needed to fling a pilot and his seat clear of a plane at various speeds, he did not know exactly how much upward compression thrust the human body could take without injury. Squadron Leader William Stewart, later Air Vice-Marshal, commandant of the Institute of Aviation Medicine, had described his experiences lying on his back on a horizontal rocket-fired trolley at Laffan's Plain, Farnborough, in which the shock of ejection was simulated by hydraulic rams. But more realistic tests, with a human subject, were now required.

By July 24, 1946, despite stern official disapproval on grounds of risk, Martin and his team felt they had solved enough problems to allow a live jump from an aircraft. Benny Lynch, who insisted on packing his own parachute and was now a veteran of scores of test shots, was delighted once again to be the star performer. Authority's fears were unfounded: flying at 320 m.p.h. in a Meteor 8,000 feet above Chalgrove aerodrome, near Benson, Oxfordshire, Lynch hauled at the face-blind and blasted himself twenty-five feet out into space. The seat worked, the back-pack parachute worked, and Lynch landed unhurt in the backyard of a public house. When the team found him he was contentedly sipping a pint of beer in the saloon bar.

A month later, he repeated the ejection at 420 m.p.h. and from 12,000 feet. It was as successful as the first. Lynch made more than thirty ejections during the development of the seat, and on only one occasion did he suffer injury—the last. He made a record jump from 30,000 feet, landed on a barbed wire fence and broke an ankle.

(Lynch, who was later awarded the British Empire Medal, has now retired from the Martin Baker company and lives in Ireland.)

At one point in the series of tests, the pilot parachute, or drogue, gave trouble. At Beaulieu and Wittering, the main parachute was released by a delayed action device set going by a static line, which also unpinned the pack flaps so that a spring could shoot out the pilot drogue. The trouble was that the drogue tended to be affected by the air turbulence round the seat after it was fired. Martin solved the problem by incorporating into the seat's design a gun and cartridge with the specific job of firing out the drogue.

In 1947 the Air Ministry recognised Martin's years of develop-ment work by making the ejection seat, and its Irvin emergency parachute, a standard fitment on all jet aircraft in the RAF and Royal Navy. This was an enormous undertaking because aircraft already in service, like the Meteor, Wyvern, Attacker, Sea Hawk and Venom, were obviously not designed to accommodate it. Apprehension from many official sources had to be dispelled: there were some pilots who regarded a cartridge under their cockpit seats as a potential hazard rather than the difference between life and death, and would surreptitiously remove it.

Much of the scepticism melted when the 'bang seat' was seen impressively to prove itself. On May 30, 1949, J. O. Lancaster, an Armstrong Whitworth test pilot, ejected himself at 3,000 feet from a prototype Flying Wing type plane when it got out of control. Lancaster landed safely, apart from a few slight injuries, as a result of what was in part a manual operation. After the seat was hurled from the aircraft, he had to unfasten his harness, thus discarding the seat, and pull the parachute ripcord—a method which made low-level escapes risky and often fatal because the parachute would fail to open in time.

By 1953 Martin was hard at work on a fully automatic system which involved no more effort on the pilot's part than pulling the protective blind over his face, thus triggering off the whole pro-cedure. He also improved his two-stage telescopic cartridge gun to give it an ejection velocity of 80 feet per second. Tests with this, coupled with a time release mechanism set at $1\frac{1}{2}$ seconds, proved that escapes could be made at low level if the aircraft were flying at not less than 90 knots.

When the time came for a live runway-level demonstration, Martin was at first forbidden, on grounds of risk, to use the Meteor he had been loaned, but later the Ministry relented and the test went ahead. At Chalgrove airfield, on September 3, 1953, Squadron Leader John Fifield ejected himself from the Meteor's rear cockpit during take-off, his parachute bearing him to earth in six seconds fully deployed, to the immense satisfaction and relief of all concerned, including himself. For this, Martin received the personal congratulations of the Air Minister. (A month earlier, a 22-year-old flying officer, Hedley Molland, became the RAF's first pilot to eject himself at speed faster than sound—from a Hawker Hunter in a steep dive at around 760 m.p.h.)

It was his progress with the low-level escapes that won Martin acceptance in the United States. The U.S. Navy first showed interest in 1946, though they obtained ejection seats from American manufacturers for some years afterwards. In 1957, however, orders reached Britain for Martin-Baker ejection seats to be installed in ten types of U.S. Navy aircraft.

Despite numerous improvements to the basic design of the seat over the years, Martin was constantly worried by the twelve per cent of pilots using it who did not survive. In terms of human lives lost, this meant an average of twenty pilots a year killed, more than half of them because of lack of height at the time of leaving the aircraft.

The problem was to give more height to the ejection seat before the parachute opened, but without placing a greater strain on the airman. Martin had already reached the limit of performance with the ejection cartridge gun, which thrust up the back of the seat. Now he tried using rockets. By placing these under the seat and directing them through its centre of gravity, he was able to give the seat more height and, by cutting the power of the cartridge charge, ensure a gentler ride. Even so, he could still achieve an acceleration figure of fifteen times the force of gravity.

Three live test ejections were made using this method in 1961, the first demonstrating its 'zero/zero' capability; that is to say, ejection at no forward speed and no height, as from a still plane on a runway. The parachutist who performed this was shot so far into the air that he was able to float down for 200 feet with his parachute canopy fully open.

The coming of Vertical Take-Off and Landing aircraft brought a new and demanding challenge. What chance would a pilot have of getting down alive from a plane like the P1127 which might, if suffering engine trouble, drop vertically and thus weaken the ejection seat's powerful thrust? Martin erected a vertical test track, vaguely reminiscent of the original test rig used by Bernard Lynch, to experiment with ejections while dropping at eighty feet per second. From the recorded findings of this exercise, Martin and his technicians spent three years perfecting an advanced kind of tailor-made escape system for the P1127.

Today, Martin's ejection seat is used in fifty air forces throughout the world. It has progressed through ten designs, the last due to be fitted in the Panavia MRCA strike aircraft in Britain, Germany and Italy. The basic principle remains: pilot and seat are fired out of the plane, the seat falls away and he lands on his parachute. But experimental work has been protracted, painstaking and complex as designs have been modified to keep pace with changes in aircraft and their capability and function.

Over the years the seat has acquired a time-release unit, to ensure that the drogue parachute transfers its pull to the main twenty-four feet canopy at just the right moment. A 'barostat' was incorporated into the seat so that the parachute would not open and keep a man lingering at very high altitudes, where extreme cold or lack of oxygen would spell certain death. This instrument, which is automatically operated by air pressure, prevents the main 'chute from opening till a certain height is reached, normally 10,000 feet. Until that point, the jumper feeds on the ejection seat's built-in supply of oxygen, which is switched on the moment he is shot out of the plane.

A barostatic control, developed earlier by Irvin's, was used to good effect over Derbyshire in April 1958, when two RAF officers, Flight Lieutenant John de Salis and Flying Officer Patrick Lowe, made the highest ever ejection seat escape. They were flying a Canberra bomber, which was specially designed to collect radioactive samples over hydrogen bomb explosions, when at 57,000 feet their plane suddenly blasted apart and they were thrown out in their ejection seats.

Their seat harnesses were unshackled and the seats dropped away. The temperature was a deadly minus 70 degrees F., and the air disastrously thin. The barostat allowed the pair to fall free for nine miles while they breathed the parachute assemblies' oxygen supply. Then, at a pre-set height of 13,000 feet, the barostat was automatically activated. The parachutes opened and, breathing easily, the two men landed frost-bitten but with only minor injuries, from which they quickly recovered.

The ejection seat has also had mechanical leg restraints introduced to stop the airman's legs flailing dangerously when the seat is fired out. And it was found that the main parachute could be opened more quickly for low level escape if extra drogue parachutes were installed to assist it. Now there are two drogues in tandem, one 22 inches in diameter (the 'controller' drogue) and a main drogue, 5 feet in diameter. This system cuts the time lag between ejection and opening the main 'chute.

Another development has ensured that the parachute and rigging lines are automatically released if a landing is made in the sea.

To make escape from low level ejections more certain, a row of between two and six rockets, with one-inch thick combustion tubes, are now installed as a matter of course under the seat to push it up to a safe level. Two-inch thick rockets are used in VTOL aircraft such as the Harrier, to counteract their tendency to drop quickly if the engine fails, rather than glide to earth like other types of aircraft. These rockets can hurl an airman as much as 450 feet into the air—more than two and a half times the height of Nelson's Column.

For seats fitted into naval aircraft, like the Buccaneer, there was an additional refinement: automatic escape from submersion after a crash into the sea. This system automatically separates the pilot from the seat and the parachute and throws him towards the surface with a fully inflated lifejacket.

Even though they use the ejection seat, not all pilots survive. The seat works and the parachute opens, but they may drown after a landing in the sea or burn to death after parachuting into the blazing wreckage of their own crashed plane.

But up to ninety-five in every hundred ejections *are* successful, and 3,400 air crew who have parachuted to safety with Sir James Martin's piece of technological wizardry have lived to tell the tale.

13

THE FUN JUMPERS

AFTER AN hour, the low mantle of strato-cumulus cloud melts reluctantly away, surrendering to blue patches of bright summer sky. An ageing De Havilland Rapide, spatted like an old gentleman from another era, circles the sky as if seeking out his favourite clubroom chair.

For a moment, the engine cuts. One . . . two . . . three . . . four tiny specks disgorge themselves from the plane like ripe peas from a pod. Within seconds, this corner of the sky is alive with a small rash of snapping canopies, yellow and blue, red-white-and-blue, yellow and red. Soon they mature into full-blown parachutes, each with a human cargo straining determinedly for the gravel target area on the ground, and more especially the beckoning white disc, no bigger than a man's hand, in the centre.

Another day in the national parachute jumping championships has begun.

In the hands of the accomplished practitioner, the sport parachute is almost a precision instrument, manufactured with a fine regard for aerodynamics and the ways in which a parachute can exploit them. It appears sometimes in guises very different from the familiar white mushroom of the emergency parachute: there are triangular canopies, heart-shaped canopies, some looking like mattresses, others slashed with a systematic arrangement of slots and skirts—all attempts to achieve maximum steerability or forward speed, or both, without sacrificing stability.

Without detracting from the inherent thrill and exhilaration of leaping into space, great emphasis in sport parachuting is always placed on the need for good quality equipment, and a strict regard for safety discipline in training, thus reducing avoidable accidents to a minimum.

Fatalities are rare, and injuries commonly no more serious than a twisted ankle or broken limb. And accidents are more often to be blamed on carelessness by the jumper than on the parachute itself, which if properly packed, should not malfunction.

But mistakes are made. Twenty-year-old Jackie Smith, the only woman member of the famous Red Devils free-fall team, was taking part in an Army tattoo at Swansea when her main parachute failed to open at 2,400 feet because a metal ripcord guide had twisted out of alignment. When she pulled the ripcord of her reserve—which every sport jumper has to carry—it opened inside out and tore halfway down. Nevertheless, she managed to make a soft, though wet, landing in the sea.

Two members of the South Staffordshire sky-diving club had narrow escapes when, during a free-fall link-up record attempt, they crashed at 10,000 feet on to an aircraft flying beneath the one from which they had dropped. One jumper came down with the plane; the other, who had landed on the tail, pushed himself off and parachuted down. Miraculously, both survived, and only suffered minor injuries.

Jumping with a parachute for fun probably really began nearly 200 years ago with André-Jacques Garnerin, though skydiving of a sort began in the 1930s, a period of much experimentation with the delayed drop and the heyday of 'bird men' such as the American, Clem Sohn. The bird men were exhibition jumpers, with canvas 'wings' webbing their outstretched arms and legs, who would leap from aircraft, then cavort about the sky until, thousands of feet later, they opened their parachutes. Sometimes. For their reckless careers tended to be short, often ending in death. In May 1936, Sohn took part in a display at Hanworth airfield, London, dropping at 10,000 feet and gliding until he was a thousand feet from the ground. He landed safely on this occasion, but less than a year later, at Vincennes, France, his parachute caught up on one of his 'wings' and did not open; nor did his reserve.

More recently, in May 1956, Leo Valentin, a 37-year-old French birdman who in his time made more than 600 parachute jumps and used 'wings' of balsa wood and alloy fitted with ailerons, was killed before a crowd of 100,000 people attending the International Air Pageant at Liverpool Airport.

Having made one thrilling delayed drop from a Dakota, Valentin went up again, but this time hit the side of the plane as he left it. Officials realised something was wrong when his parachute began to open after only 1,000 feet of free-fall. But it failed to deploy properly and Valentin dropped helplessly through space; he was killed outright two miles from the airfield.

A serious attempt at high altitude free-fall was part of a U.S. Air Force research project in 1960 which resulted in a remarkable world record for the courageous officer, Captain Joseph W. Kittinger. On August 16, he left Holloman Base in New Mexico in the gondola of a helium balloon and jumped out at 102,000 feet, a height which gave him an uninterrupted view of the earth's surface for 400 miles.

Kittinger, though he at times experienced a choking sensation, was in control of all his faculties during his fall. The free-fall drop of 84,000 feet was made with the aid of a stabilising drogue, and his barostatically controlled main parachute opened at 17,500 feet after the four-and-a-half minute plunge through space. Captain Kittinger's record remains unbroken at the time of writing.

Flamboyant exhibitionism of the 'bird-man' type has given way now to exacting exercises in accuracy and style, with competition rules laid down for world championship jumping by the Fédération Aeronautique Internationale, and in the U.K. by the British Parachute Association, which is the sport's controlling body and is responsible for organising training and insisting on minimum safety requirements.

Accurate parachute jumping demands keen judgment and knowledge, gained through training and experience, of a parachute's capabilities as a 'vehicle', which will glide, with a forward speed of perhaps 12 m.p.h. and can be braked and steered at will.

The canopy nylon of the sport parachute is more tightly woven than that of the emergency version, making the cloth less porous. The air that would have permeated the canopy is forced out, in descent, through a series of slots, producing a mild form of jet propulsion. By manipulating the toggles attached to the parachute's rigging lines, a highly skilled jumper can steer himself to the target with great precision.

Accuracy parachuting is largely a participant sport. From the spectator's standpoint the gentle swaying of the parachutist as he glides earthwards, and the soft swish of the canopy, help to make the procedure look deceptively easy. In individual and team-of-four events, contestants must jump from an aircraft and land as close as possible to a white disc ten centimetres in diameter, on the ground. In the British National Parachuting Championships the jumping height is fixed at 700 metres, parachute opening being delayed for up to three seconds after leaving the plane. Distances landed from the target spot are measured for each competitor's jumps and totalled. The competitor, or team, with the smallest total distance, wins.

Style jumping, on the other hand, is a test of individual achievement in which accuracy of landing plays only a minor role. The skill lies in performing a number of manoeuvres during the free-fall drop after leaving the aircraft and on reaching the maximum possible speed of descent—between 120 m.p.h. and 160 m.p.h., depending on the mid-air posture. Unlike the parachute used in accuracy events, the one in this case has one main purpose—to set the jumper down safely after his manoeuvres.

In the British championships the stylist leaps from about 2,000 metres, and he must not delay the opening of his parachute for more than twenty-five seconds. When he leaves the plane, he stabilises himself in a 'frog' or semi-spreadeagled position, then moves into a programme of barrel rolls, 360-degree turns and forward and backward loops. Points are awarded for speed and precision and deducted for unfinished or incorrect manoeuvres.

Out of style jumping by individual parachutists was born the kind of free-fall activity known as 'relative work'. This is the spectacular process of forming patterns in the air with several jumpers. Gliding towards each other, or 'tracking' as it is officially called, the skydivers join hands to form circles, or 'stars', in ever increasing numbers. United States jumpers have repeatedly set up new records for stars; currently, their score stands at an impressive twenty-six.

The first world parachuting championships were held (unofficially) by a band of zealots in Yugoslavia in 1951, with five nations competing. The championships were recognised by the F.A.I. three years later and have been held in alternate years ever since. In the 1972 event, Britain's team was placed seventh out of the twenty-nine participating nations, top honours going to the U.S.S.R., with the United States second and Czechoslovakia third. The winning individual stylist was a Frenchman, and in the team accuracy event Britain narrowly missed winning a medal by slipping finally into fourth place. The winners were Switzerland with the U.S.S.R. runners-up and Czechoslovakia once again third.

The latest championships strengthened a widely held feeling that because jumpers have become so expert, and their parachutes so sophisticated, new and more challenging forms of competition should be added to the programme. In the accuracy event, distances from the target disc, once a matter of feet, are now a question of centimetres; and 'dead centres', where the jumper actually lands on the disc, are becoming commonplace.

A likely development in future championships would seem to be the introduction of the dauntingly named 'sequential relative work', which is the performance of a set number of prescribed movements, possibly against the clock, or even timed link-ups.

But the mass of parachutists find abundant thrills in non-competitive jumping at club level. Nearly 12,000 of them have passed through membership of the British Parachute Association[1] which, formed in 1962, is now 4,000 strong (200 of them women) and expanding at the rate of about ten per cent a year. At one time, servicemen predominated the membership, but now the balance has swung over to civilians.

Much of parachuting's progress as a sport has been due to commercial patronage. The original promotion work was largely

[1] The British Parachute Association (Secretary-General, Squadron Leader W. Paul), Artillery Mansions, 75 Victoria Street, London SW1 0HW.

carried out by one national newspaper, the *Daily Telegraph*, which has also presented a number of valuable trophies for annual competition; latterly, the Target trust group has given a helping hand, by sponsoring the British national team for the first time, in 1972.

To share the excitement of competition, or indeed sport parachuting at all, membership of the British Parachute Association and one of the 32 clubs is essential. The B.P.A. is recognised by the Civil Aviation Authority as the governing body of the sport. The C.A.A. grants to parachute clubs block exemption from the provisions of the Air Navigation Order 1970, which prohibits pilots from dropping anything or anybody from an aircraft other than in an emergency.

Also, the B.P.A. holds a block insurance policy covering every individual member up to a sum of £100,000 including third party and member-to-member. The £4 annual subscription to the B.P.A., which is in addition to the club subscription, includes the cost of insurance and the Association's bi-montly journal, *Sport Parachutist*.

Before he can start, the tenderfoot parachutist must be able to produce a fitness certificate from his doctor. Only then can he begin the six to twelve hours of ground training and take the prescribed six static line jumps which precede the first free-fall drop. Basic courses can be arranged to cover a long weekend at a cost of about £16.50, which includes the training itself, loan of parachute, cost of the first descent and a year's membership of the B.P.A.

During the course, there will be instruction on the principles of stability, canopy control, landings, malfunctions and emergency action, parachute packing and aircraft drill. All the beginner has to provide in the way of equipment are a white boiler suit or overalls, crash helmet and rubber-soled boots.

The most expensive item of equipment is of course the parachute itself, though carefully looked after it will last for years and be good for up to 1,000 jumps. Parachutes are made by the American Pioneer Company, which makes the Para-Commander,

Irvin Great Britain Ltd (the Delta II Parawing and Skydriver), and RFD-GQ (the Pathfinder). The Para-Commander is probably the most popular sport parachute in Europe and America and, including harness, costs about £300. But the student parachutist could kit himself out with second-hand equipment for little more than £70.

An example of what sound training and persistence can achieve in sport parachute competitions is typified by John Meacock, who runs the Peterborough Parachute Centre at Sibson Airfield, Huntingdonshire. Now a veteran of more than 2,400 jumps, Meacock took up the sport in 1963, and three years later won the Army championship. In 1969 he became British national champion for the first time, since when he has won the title twice.

The advent of multiple aerofoil parachutes has led to a challenging new kind of fun-jumping—parascending, which is enjoying increasing popularity among children as well as adults.

Parascending is practised at sea as well as on land. One girl, towed by motor boat, travelled more than half-way across the English Channel by parachute. On land, the parachutist takes off with the aid of a towing vehicle, such as a Land-Rover. The parachute's canopy is opened out on the ground by two holders. The truck takes up tension and the canopy is allowed to fill with air, and the lift then created allows the parachutist to rise. Experienced practitioners release themselves at, say, 1,200 feet and then perhaps embark on some of the exercises followed by aircraft jumpers.

The parachute was first developed for ascent in 1918, for lifting an observer behind a U-boat. Parascending made its first appearance in Britain in 1962, and has gained a firm foothold in the sporting world, with fifty-four clubs—thirty-four military and twenty civilian.

14

OUT OF THIS WORLD

W HEN HE was Prince of Wales, the late Duke of Windsor often flew with the RAF. One day, when he was being helped into his parachute harness before a flight, somebody asked him if he knew how to use it. 'No,' he answered, 'and I don't want to.'

If the Prince thought that a little knowledge might tempt Providence into giving him cause to use it, he need not have worried; he never had to. Thirty years later, however, his successor, Prince Charles, had no qualms at all, and in an age which allows Royalty a greater scope for adventure than it has had for centuries, he jumped from 1,200 feet with the PXI Mark 4, the standard military parachute designed for paratroops. Lacking experience, he caught his legs in the rigging lines, but fortunately disentangled them without trouble and splashed down in the sea off the Dorset coast.

Although paratroop training methods and equipment have not changed in essence in thirty years, they have done so in important details. Irvin's PX parachute is bigger than the old 'X' type – 32 feet in flat diameter instead of 28, thus giving a slower, steadier drop. It is now fitted with a 14-inch net skirt, which successfully prevents blown peripheries, a type of malfunction causing part of the canopy to twist inside out and produce dangerously rapid descents. Also, since 1955, every paratrooper has carried an RFD-GQ reserve parachute.

No. 1 Parachute Training School, formerly at Ringway, puts second-generation professional paratroops, Territorials and foreign trainees through their paces with a four weeks' basic course in parachuting at Abingdon, Berkshire. Gone is the cramped old 10-man Whitley bomber for training jumps, and the more amenable 20-man Dakota; 62 paratroops now pack comfortably into the newer Hercules transport aircraft, which can discharge its parachutists at twice the previous rate.

In a huge hangar, recruits are literally given a firm grounding in aircraft drill, flight and landing techniques with the aid of harnesses suspended from the roof and mock-ups of fuselages, jumping platforms and balloon cages. Here discipline is firmly and wisely maintained. Through the hubbub of shouted orders, the message is the School's motto, 'Knowledge Dispels Fear', and the N.C.O. instructors, furnished by the RAF as always, are anxious to instil confidence, not to unnerve or humiliate.

During the ensuing weeks the initial ordeal of jumping must be faced and overcome, a private challenge which sometimes proves too much, for there are some who refuse to jump. While under training, refusal is not considered the offence it would be for a fully-fledged paratrooper; but nor, in deference to his own safety and that of his later companions, is he given a second chance. He is quietly returned to his original unit, with no hard feelings.

The course consists of two static line jumps from the cage of a captive balloon, swaying on its cable 800 feet up, six descents from an aircraft, including one at night, and two drops with equipment —a total burden for the parachute of more than 300 pounds. The jumper's equipment is suspended below him, so that in hitting the ground first it momentarily checks the rate of his fall.

In the future, the sport parachute's gliding characteristics may well be exploited militarily, units like the Special Air Service making 'stand off' drops of small patrols to work behind enemy lines. The paratroops would sky-dive together as soon as they left their plane, descending the rest of the way on steerable parachutes. These would enable them to glide horizontally three or four times the height from which they dropped, and either rendezvous secretly or take the enemy by surprise in complete silence.

For mass drops, aircraft would fly in at treetop height, thus escaping radar detection. Then at the last minute they would climb quickly to 800 or 1,000 feet and drop their paratroops by static line.

Whatever a parachute's purpose and whoever is destined to use it, intensive efforts are made as a matter of course to ensure it is fit for its job. No visitor to a parachute factory can fail to be impressed by two things: first, its silence; second, a paramount preoccupation with safety.

The Government, for its part, insists on high standards. Each parachute company must employ an inspectorate, headed by a chief inspector himself approved by the Defence Quality Assurance Board. On his staff is a team of inspectors totalling around twenty per cent of the entire factory working strength, who implement a programme of stringent tests and spot checks right down the production line.

Is the canopy fabric of the right porosity and tensile strength? Are the emergency parachute's 24 gores and 96 panels firmly sewn? Are the rigging lines the prescribed length measured at the correct tension? Is the parachute well packed, the rigging lines evenly looped, the ripcord properly set? Has a thorough job been made of the repair to that torn parachute? Check . . . counter-check. Tested and approved; and the proud boast, confidently asserted, that 'we have never had any fatality due to bad work-manship or incorrect manufacture'.

In basic design, the emergency parachute has changed little over the years, except that faster aircraft have made it necessary to use it in conjunction with an ejection seat, already described. Also, parachutes are no longer produced in white only. N.A.T.O. air forces colour them in four vertical segments from apex to hem: khaki, sand, white and international orange. So on landing, the pilot can either camouflage his presence or make himself con-spicuous, depending on circumstances and terrain, by laying the parachute on the ground with the appropriate colour uppermost. The Royal Navy prefers yellow parachutes for quicker identifica-tion at sea.

Since the parachute was officially adopted by the Government for the RAF in the 1920s, it has made few inroads into civil aviation. The arguments against it are admittedly formidable. A parachute for every passenger would add enormously to the total weight carried. Passengers would not be trained in their use. And if they did know how to use them, there would be an impossible scramble at the exits. Moreover, because most civil air accidents occur on take-off or landing, a parachute would be of little help anyway. Test pilots apart, civil air crews are not equipped with parachutes, on the grounds that it would be unfair to supply them while passengers went without.

Light aircraft pilots who carry parachutes are the exception rather than the rule; many small planes are not designed to accommodate them, though the standard emergency 'chute has been adapted to form special flat packs to help overcome this. Most of Britain's 7,000 gliding enthusiasts fly with parachutes as a matter of long-standing habit, and in gliders intended for cloud flying and aerobatic manoeuvres, provision for parachutes is essential for an airworthiness certificate.

In the United States it has not escaped notice that advances which have produced aircraft capable of carrying more than 300 passengers have left escape methods lagging behind. One idea engaging U.S. Air Force researchers is that of building strips of explosive 'detonating cord' and cutters into the fuselage round emergency exits, which in the event of a crash landing would immediately blast open.

More ambitious and futuristic is a suggestion to use the cord in conjunction with parachutes for accidents in flight. The cord would 'parcel' the plane at intervals all round the fuselage. If the aircraft were in jeopardy, a handle would be pulled by the pilot or a member of the crew and the detonating cord explode, slicing the fuselage into neat segments, each of which would carry passengers down on its own parachute.

From time to time attempts have been made to go the whole way and lower an entire aircraft by parachute to avoid a crash. As far back as 1910, J. F. Webb took out a British patent for a huge triple assembly of parachutes, to be deployed one after the other by an 'air anchor'—a kind of large dome-like auxiliary parachute. Suspended beneath this bizarre contrivance was the aircraft. Whether Webb's device worked or not is unknown, but eighteen years later a single parachute 84 feet in diameter and strong enough to support a loaded plane was developed by the U.S. Air Corps.

Modern aircraft would probably be too heavy for any parachute small enough to be carried in the fuselage, but pressure-packed parachutes made of ribbon strips are used to recover pilotless target or reconnaissance 'drones' after they have run out of fuel or finished their job. Parachutes also bring down guided missiles at the research and development stage, a system first used by the Germans during tests on their secret weapon, the V-2 rocket bomb, in 1943.

For aircraft, the parachute is more gainfully employed as a braking device, one of three methods used to shorten the long landing run needed by high-speed planes, at the same time preventing wear on brakes and tyres. Some aircraft, for example, on naval carriers, use arrester hooks on landing. Some have reverse thrust engines; but these of course add greatly to weight, and a brake parachute is a light and effective alternative.

A canopy 31 feet in flat diameter was used on the prototype Concorde in the development stage. Parachutes are also used to brake the Caravelle, a commercial plane, V-bombers Victor and Vulcan, and strike and fighter planes like the Hunter, Jaguar, Lightning and Phantom.

The canopies of many brake parachutes are fashioned of lengths of strong nylon ribbon stitched into concentric circles, with a gap between each. It is strong enough to withstand the enormous opening shock without damage, and will maintain its stability even if wet, when the fabric's porosity is reduced almost to nil. A small spring-loaded auxiliary 'chute helps rapid deployment.

Versions of the brake parachute are used by racing cars, particularly dragsters, which need to slow from 140-60 m.p.h. That Arnold Sundqvist, a 26-year-old Swedish jet car driver, is alive today is due to his parachutes. During a run-up to a flying quarter-mile during the World Speed Record Weekend at Elvington, Yorkshire, in October 1972, he was travelling at 300 m.p.h. when he swerved, ran off the runway for half a mile and crashed, slowing down as he did so. 'It was my two parachutes which saved me,' he said afterwards.

The parachute's retarding quality brings aircraft out of spins during testing, thus saving the lives of pilots and thousands of pounds in the cost of the plane. Normally an anti-spin parachute is assisted out of the rear of the fuselage by means of a gun. A steel slug is shot out at an angle, away from the air turbulence, taking with it an auxiliary 'chute which pulls out the main canopy on a long strop. When the plane emerges from its stall, goes into a steep dive and is thus under control, the parachute can be immediately cut loose.

As an alternative to conventional and expensive pilotless aircraft as missile targets, Irvin's developed a system using a supply container (as ballast) attached to a slow-falling parachute as used for dropping flares. The unique feature of this type is that the canopy is silverised so that it can be tracked by radar.

A similar version helps the Meteorological Office to keep a close watch on weather conditions in the stratosphere. Rocket-sonde parachutes have since 1963 been fired from a station in South Uist, in the Outer Hebrides, which receives data on temperature and winds.

A solid-propellant rocket, about eight feet long, is fired to an average height of forty-five miles. At its highest point, a small explosive charge forces off the nose cone, liberating a 15-foot-diameter parachute, which carries a sensor and a low-powered transmitter. The parachute canopy is of fine silk so that it can be packed into as small a container as possible. Its thirty-two shaped gores are coated alternately with silverised copper finish, enabling the parachute to be followed by radar up to seventy-five miles away. From its drift as it descends, the wind direction can be calculated.

The sensor, as its name indicates, is sensitive to changes in temperature. As the temperature changes, so does the pitch of its radio signal, which is picked up by receivers on the ground.

These parachute rockets are fired regularly from a network of stations mainly in the earth's northern hemisphere. From the data they collect, meteorologists can chart patterns of weather behaviour at various heights above the earth and discover the causes of stratospheric disturbances, some of which are very severe, particularly in winter.

Since the 1930s, new jobs have been found for man-carrying parachutes. The Russians, quicker than most to realise the parachute's potentialities, established a 20-man medical team to drop into remote areas of the country with personnel and supplies, and their example has since been followed in hitherto inaccessible spots all over the world.

The vast forest lands of the western United States have seen the development of a great team of 'smoke-jumpers', who act as shock troops in damping down timber fires before they gain too devastating a hold. Even in the early days of their existence, the smoke-jumpers were saving three times their cost.

These men, fully equipped and highly trained, number well over 400, and have more than 100,000 individual jumps to their credit. Their planes are well-equipped too, with devices like 'mini-scanners' to detect, by means of infra-red rays, small fires which are not betrayed by smoke.

The smoke-jumper's parachute, the T-10, has been adapted from a paratroop type. It is slotted vertically and lobed at the rear, to make it highly manoeuvrable. The descending jumper, who also carries a reserve parachute, can travel forwards at 8 m.p.h. and by hauling on his control lines rotate himself completely in as little as eight seconds. The main canopy is 32 feet in diameter, about the same as a paratrooper's, and is similarly operated by static line. He also carries a 24-foot emergency 'chute on every jump.

These fire-fighters have had their share of tragedy. In 1949, twelve smoke-jumpers and a district guard were burned to death in a blaze in the Helena Forest. But such is the efficiency of their parachute that only one death has occurred as a result of the jump itself.

Over ten years, parachutes have been used by the Post Office, Cable & Wireless, and Standard Telephones and Cables in laying international telephone cables under the sea. The parachute, made by RFD-GQ, helped to lower to the ocean bed a ten-foot-long, torpedo-shaped device called a repeater, which was installed in the cable every twenty-five miles or so to boost telephone messages. Consisting of amplification devices protected by a metal casing, the repeater was heavier than the cable and had to be slowed to keep pace with it as it sank after being paid out at the stern of the laying ship.

The parachute canopy, of red rayon and about 14 feet in 'flying' diameter, was tugged out of its bag by the repeater as it flopped into the water. The 'chute began to deploy immediately and was freed from its cargo by a hydrostatic release at a pre-determined depth. The repeater sank to its place on the ocean bed perhaps 3,500 fathoms below.

About 1,500 parachutes have been put to this use by British companies in various parts of the world. The American Telephone & Telegraph Co. employed similar techniques in laying various American-designed cable systems.

The idea of using parachutes in water is not a new one. Hugh Bell visualised an umbrella-like 'water grapnel', as he called it, a kind of braking device for his aerostatic invention of 1848, as mentioned earlier.

In the 'seventies, there is still a big call for supply-dropping parachutes. They are extremely versatile and often immense: the biggest has touched 200 feet in diameter. Depending on the size of the load, supply parachutes may be dropped in clusters for stability. Loads range from bicycles to lifeboats, vehicles, artillery and heavy oil surveying equipment. Ten tons' worth of goods on a cluster is not uncommon. The biggest single parachute load was of more than twenty-two tons of steel plates dropped from a U.S. Hercules aircraft on six parachutes in California in 1970.

Supply parachutes are made of nylon, cotton or cheap synthetic fibre. The British RFD-GQ company has even produced a strange-looking version in the shape of a cross and made of polypropylene. It is cheap enough to be sold as 'disposable', though in practice it can be used many times over.

In contrast to this simple parachute is an advanced one developed by Irvin in Canada for tactical airborne troop supply in high level drops. The parachute canopy is reefed round its skirt to prevent it from opening until it has reached a low level. A radar altimeter automatically disreefs the parachute at a programmed height so that it can bring the cargo to a gentle touchdown.

Since the earliest days when man ventured beyond the bounds of the earth, the parachute has been his constant companion, unseen on the journey except to swing him back down through the atmosphere to a safe homecoming on land or water. All the manned spaceflight programmes, Russian as well as American, have depended on the parachute in the final stages, even though their methods of using it have differed slightly.

When Yuri Gagarin, the world's first cosmonaut, made his first 90-minute circuit of the earth in spaceship Vostok I in 1961, he remained in the capsule after re-entry and came down with it suspended on a parachute. Four months later another system was tried. Major Gherman Titov, in Vostok II, was flung out through an escape hatch with a rocket-powered ejection seat and came down by parachute like an escaping airman—the method adopted for subsequent Russian space missions, all of which have concluded on *terra firma*, not in the sea.

A parachute fault killed one of the Russian cosmonauts in 1967. Colonel Vladimir Komarov, the only occupant of Soyuz ('Union') I, blasted off from Russia uneventfully early in the morning of April 23 and was soon beaming back optimistic reports on conditions and his state of health. For the next twenty-four hours all continued to go well. Then came re-entry, and disaster. His main parachute's rigging lines became entangled only four miles above the earth and he died, a martyr to a million-to-one misfortune.

The United States' Mercury, Gemini and Apollo capsules have all returned to splashdowns in the sea. Because of the water's cushioning effect, smaller parachutes could be used and the descent made at a higher speed than on land. Ejection seats would only have been activated had there been a mishap resulting in an off-the-launching-pad abort. Gemini's ejection seat would have shot the astronaut 900 feet across the launching site and landed him on his emergency parachute in about twenty seconds.

For higher altitude ejection, a 'ballute' (a self-inflated, air-filled, cone-shaped balloon-cum-parachute) would have helped to stabilise the astronaut after the seat had fallen away and until the main 'chute filled out. For the splashdown, Mercury and Gemini capsules each came down on one parachute. Apollo was given three giant orange-and-white striped parachutes which opened out in the last stage of an automatic landing process which, viewed on the television screen, seemed as straightforward as pulling a ripcord. In fact, the whole operation was a masterpiece of techno-logical expertise and ingenious stowage.

Upon the trio of parachutes rested the entire responsibility of slowing the command module from 300 m.p.h. to a mere 22 m.p.h. when it hit the sea. At 23,000 feet, two white nylon conical ribbon 'chutes, somewhat smaller than the RAF emergency type, blossomed out, followed by three white nylon ring-slot canopies, each about 7 feet in diameter. At 10,000 feet these in turn hauled out the huge 84-foot main ring-sail parachutes. These, developed by an American company, Northrop Ventura, were similar to ring-slot 'chutes, but the concentric circles of fabric were fashioned into billowing vents, for increased stability, which were similar in shape to the sails on a square-rigged ship.

The progressive deployment of all these parachutes was trig-gered off automatically by four barometric switches and time delay devices, which ensured that the parachutes burst open at exactly the correct height and moment.

There could easily have been a disaster involving parachutes during the Apollo 15 mission in 1971. As the spacecraft Endeavour plunged down through the earth's atmosphere on its homeward journey, astronauts James Irwin, David Scott and Alfred Worden, inside the command module, realised that only two of the three parachutes had developed; the canopy of the third dragged flaccidly above but did not inflate. 'Be prepared for a hard impact!' they were warned.

One reason for the failure of the third parachute was that during the module's re-entry, highly inflammable fuel was jettisoned from a hot nozzle (a practice abandoned in later missions) and damaged the rigging lines of the parachute.

Fortunately for the space men, however, there was a built-in safety margin. The system was designed to land them, if a trifle more quickly, on only two parachutes. So they, and their precious $1\frac{1}{2}$ hundred-weights of moon rocks, were secure.

With the end of the Apollo programme, the moon ceases to be man's cosmic objective. But there will be other worlds to explore, if not to conquer, less barren and perhaps with atmospheres dense enough to support parachute landings, such as Russia's Venus project with Venera-4.

For the story of the parachute is not yet over, nor perhaps will it ever be, as long as man seeks to explore space and afterwards return home. For as far as one can foresee, the angel's wing of the parachute will be there to set him down. That this is possible at all is a proud tribute to those whose names are landmarks in the 200-year-old story of the parachute: men like Garnerin, Cocking, Hampton and Broadwick, Calthrop, Orde-Lees and Irvin, whose faith in the big umbrella was paralleled only by a similar burning faith in themselves.

BIBLIOGRAPHY

Bennett, Air Vice-Marshal D. C. T., *Path Finder* (Muller, 1958).
Brickhill, Paul, *Reach For the Sky* (Collins, 1954).
Brown, W. D., *Parachutes* (Pitman, 1951).
Burbidge, William F., *From Balloon to Bomber* (John Crowther, 1946).
Caidin, Martin, *The Silken Angels* (Lippincott, 1964).
Lord Douglas of Kirtleside and Wright, R. C., *Years of Command* (Collins, 1963).
Dwiggins, Don, *The Story of Parachuting and Skydiving* (Collier-Macmillan, 1969).
Foot, M. R. D., *S.O.E. in France* (H.M.S.O., 1962).
Gatland, Kenneth, *Manned Spaceflight* (Blandford, 1971).
Gibbs-Smith, Charles H., *The Aeroplane: An Historical Survey* (H.M.S.O., 1960).
Gibbs-Smith, Charles H., *Sir George Cayley's Aeronautics* (H.M.S.O., 1962).
Hodgson, J. E., *History of Aeronautics in Great Britain* (Oxford University Press, 1924).
Holt, L. T. C., *The Aeronauts* (Longman, 1966).
Jones, H. A., *War in the Air* (Oxford University Press, 1937).
Low, Professor A. M., *Parachutes in Peace and War* (Scientific Book Club, 1942).
Lindbergh, Charles, *We—Pilot and Plane* (G. P. Putnam's Sons, 1927).
Mackersey, Ian, *Into the Silk* (Robert Hale, 1956).
Neumann, G. P., *The German Air Force in the Great War* (Hodder, 1920).
Newnham, Maurice, *Prelude to Glory* (Sampson Low, 1947).
Saunders, H. St George, *The Red Beret* (Michael Joseph, 1949).
Slim, Field Marshal Sir William, *Defeat Into Victory* (Cassell, 1957).
Spaight, J. M., *Air Power and War Rights* (Longman, 1947).
Tranum, John, *Nine Lives* (John Hamilton, 1933).
Wedgwood Benn, Captain W., *In the Sideshows* (Hodder, 1919).
Wilkinson, Stephen, *Lighter Than Air* (A. H. Stockwell, 1930).

Willans, T. W., *Parachuting and Skydiving* (Faber, 1964).

Periodicals:
Flight International (formerly *Flight*).
Royal Aeronautical Society Journal.
Mechanics' Magazine (1823–1872).

INDEX

Women's Auxiliary Air Force, 103
Woods-Scawen, Tony, 115–16
Worden, Alfred, 147
World's Fair at San Francisco, 43
World Speed Record Weekend, 142
World War I, 54–71, 84
World War II, 98–121
Wright, Orville and Wilbur, 42

Wright biplane, 50, 57
Wyvern plane, 127

YEARS OF COMBAT (LORD DOUGLAS), 55
York, Duke of, 16–17
Yugoslavia, 135

ZODIAC BALLOON, 31